Cyclades Islands Travel 2025

A Journey Through Greece's Landscapes, and

Dexter Tillery

Copyright © 2025 Dexter Tillery.

All rights reserved.

No part of this book may be reproduced, stored in a retrieval system, or transmitted in any form or by any means—electronic, mechanical, photocopying, recording, or otherwise—without the prior written permission of the publisher, except for the inclusion of brief quotations in a review.

Image credit

Unsplash.com

Disclaimer

This book is a work of nonfiction. The information contained within is based on the author's research and experience. The author and publisher have made every effort to ensure that the information in this book was correct at the time of publication. However, the author and publisher do not assume and hereby disclaim any liability to any party for any loss, damage, or disruption caused by errors or omissions, whether such errors or omissions result from negligence, accident, or any other cause.

DexTravel GUIDE

TABLE OF CONTENTS

INTRODUCTION: WELCOME TO THE CYCLADES — 2

- Setting the Scene: The Islands Awaken — 2
- Why the Cyclades Should Be on Your 2025 Travel List — 3
- How to Get There: From Athens to Island Hopping — 5
- 10 Fascinating Facts — 9

CHAPTER 1 — 12

SANTORINI – THE ISLAND OF DREAMS — 12

- Mesmerizing Sunsets at Oia — 12
- Discovering the Black Sand Beaches — 13
- Exploring Ancient Akrotiri: A Window into the Past — 15
- Where to Eat, Stay, and Play: Insider Tips — 18

CHAPTER 2 — 26

MYKONOS – A GLIMPSE OF GLAMOUR — 26

- Wandering the Maze of Mykonos Town — 26
- The Iconic Windmills and Little Venice — 28
- A Nightlife Like No Other: Bars, Clubs, and Beach Parties — 30
- Relaxing Beach Vibes: Psarou, Paradise, and Beyond — 34

CHAPTER 3 — 38

PAROS – SERENITY IN SIMPLICITY — 38

- The Charm of Naoussa and Parikia — 39
- Hidden Beaches and Crystal-Clear Waters — 40
- Cycling Through Ancient Villages and Olive Groves — 42
- Local Food Secrets: Where to Find the Best Souvlaki — 44

CHAPTER 4 — 50

NAXOS – THE HEART OF THE CYCLADES — 50

- Ancient Temples and the Portara: A Historical Journey 51
- Naxian Cuisine: From Kitron to Fresh Seafood 52
- Hiking the Mountains and Exploring Hidden Valleys 56
- Relaxation in the Quiet Villages: A Local's Perspective 60

CHAPTER 5 66

MILOS – THE ISLAND OF COLOR 66

- The Stunning Beaches of Sarakiniko and Firiplaka 66
- The Ancient Catacombs and Roman Theater 69
- Secluded Caves and Cliffside Villages: Uncovering Milos' Secrets 71
- Sailing Around the Island: Exploring by Boat 75

CHAPTER 6 80

SYROS – THE CULTURAL HUB 80

- Ermoupoli: The Fusion of Neoclassical and Cycladic Architecture 80
- Museums, Art Galleries, and Theatres 81
- Quiet Cafes and Artisan Shops: A Taste of Local Life 86
- Exploring the Byzantine Pathways: Walking Through History 90

CHAPTER 7 94

AMORGOS – A TRANQUIL ESCAPE 94

- The Monastery of Hozoviotissa: An Aerial Sanctuary 94
- Beaches of Amorgos: From Agia Anna to Kalotaritissa 96
- Hiking Trails Through Wild Nature: A Nature Lover's Dream 100
- Enjoying Amorgos' Slow Pace of Life 104

CHAPTER 8 110

THE LESSER-KNOWN 110

    Ios: A Hidden Gem for Hiking and Beaches 110
    Folegandros: Untouched Beauty and Hidden Coves 113
    Serifos: A Remote Paradise for Adventurers 116

CHAPTER 9 122

PRACTICAL TRAVEL TIPS FOR CYCLADES ISLANDS 122

    Getting Around: Ferries, Boats, and Private Transfers 122
    Best Time to Visit: Weather, Festivals, and Local Events 124
    What to Pack: Essentials for Island Hopping 128
    Local Customs and Etiquette to Know Before You Go 132

CONCLUSION 138

BONUS 140

5-DAY CYCLADES ISLANDS ITINERARY: EXPLORING THE BEAUTY, CULTURE, AND TRANQUILITY 140

Image by Yorgos Triantafyllou on Unsplash | Aigiali, Amorgos, Cyclades, Greece

Image by Despina Galani on Unsplash | Kleftiko, Milos island.

Image by Despina Galani on Unsplash | highest point in Serifos Chora

Image by Despina Galani on Unsplash | Hora square in Serifos

Image by Apostolis Michailidis on Unsplash | A hill with a village

Image by Despina Galani on Unsplash | Kimolos

Introduction: Welcome to the Cyclades

Setting the Scene: The Islands Awaken

As your ferry pulls into the bustling port of Santorini, a gentle breeze sweeps through the air, carrying with it the salty scent of the Aegean Sea. The islands of the Cyclades are alive with color, the whitewashed buildings gleaming under the Mediterranean sun, and the clear blue waters stretching out to the horizon. This is no mere destination; this is a place where time seems to slow down, and the timeless beauty of the landscape takes center stage.

The islands themselves feel like they've been plucked from a postcard, but in reality, they hold centuries of history, culture, and adventure. From the volcanic islands of Santorini, where fiery cliffs meet turquoise seas, to the ancient ruins of Delos, where myths and legends come to life, each island is a unique chapter in the story of Greece. The Cyclades are where nature, history, and culture converge to create an experience unlike any other. The islands awaken as early morning sunlight dances over the rippling waves, and the warmth of the day brings the islands to life with bustling markets, open-air cafés, and a vibrant nightlife that thrives well into the night.

In the Cyclades, every step you take feels like you're walking through a dream. The beauty of the landscape, the rhythm of island life, and the deep connection to Greek tradition create a harmony that resonates deeply within anyone who visits. The islands pulse with life, and yet there's a serenity that envelops you, inviting you to slow down, breathe deeply, and immerse yourself fully in the experience.

Let the islands of the Cyclades awaken your senses, as the light, colors, and sounds pull you into a world of infinite beauty.

Why the Cyclades Should Be on Your 2025 Travel List

The Cyclades are a dream come true for travelers seeking a perfect blend of history, culture, nature, and modern luxuries. Whether you're a history buff, a foodie, a beach lover, or someone who simply craves a quiet escape, these islands offer something for every type of traveler.

Breathtaking Natural Beauty

The Cyclades' landscape is a painter's palette of vibrant blues and whites, where dramatic cliffs plunge into sparkling azure waters. Imagine standing on the edge of a caldera in Santorini, watching the sun dip below the horizon, or walking along the winding cobblestone streets of Mykonos, framed by whitewashed houses with blue shutters. It's not just a vacation; it's a journey into nature's most beautiful creations.

Rich History and Ancient Wonders

Each island in the Cyclades tells a story of ancient civilizations, from the Minoans of Santorini to the ancient temples of Delos, the birthplace of Apollo. The archaeological sites here are some of the most fascinating in Greece, offering a chance to walk in the footsteps of the ancient gods. The sense of history you feel when you visit these islands is tangible—this is where legends were born.

Culinary Delights

For food lovers, the Cyclades are a culinary haven. From fresh seafood and local cheeses to unique island wines, the flavors here are as rich and diverse as the islands themselves. Don't miss out on tasting the famous Santorini tomatoes, or the Naxian potatoes, which are renowned for their flavor. The Greek meze culture will tempt your palate with an array of small, delicious dishes that are perfect for sharing.

Vibrant Culture and Traditions

The Cyclades are also rich in cultural heritage, where every island has its own unique character. From the lively nightlife of Mykonos to the tranquil, traditional villages of Paros, there is a place to suit your vibe. You'll encounter vibrant festivals, music, and dances, and the chance to witness how Greek traditions continue to thrive in the face of modernity. The locals are known for their warm hospitality, eager to share their stories and traditions with you.

Ideal for Island Hopping

The Cyclades are an archipelago, making them the perfect destination for island hopping. With each island offering something different, you can explore multiple locations in one trip. Whether you're visiting the beaches of Milos, the charming streets of Syros, or the rugged beauty of Naxos, the islands are all easily accessible by ferry, allowing you to tailor your trip to your interests.

A Place to Relax and Recharge

In a world where it's easy to get caught up in the hustle and bustle, the Cyclades offer a much-needed escape. The islands have a way of slowing you down, inviting you to relax, take in the scenery, and rejuvenate your mind and body. With crystal-clear waters, relaxing beach resorts, and a laid-back atmosphere, the Cyclades offer the perfect sanctuary for those looking to disconnect from the noise of everyday life.

2025 is the perfect year to immerse yourself in the charm of the Cyclades. Whether you're seeking adventure, relaxation, or cultural enrichment, these islands promise an unforgettable experience. From the captivating scenery to the rich traditions and the incredible people, the Cyclades will capture your heart and stay with you long after you've left.

How to Get There: From Athens to Island Hopping

Getting to the Cyclades from Athens is straightforward, with a variety of transportation options that allow you to explore these stunning islands at your own pace. Whether you're looking for speed, comfort, or a touch of adventure, the journey to the Cyclades is just as exciting as the destination itself.

By Ferry: The Traditional Way to Travel

The most popular and scenic way to get from Athens to the Cyclades is by ferry. Ferries depart regularly from the Piraeus Port, which is about 30 minutes from downtown Athens. This is the main departure point for the majority of ferries to the islands. Depending on the route and the island you're heading to, the ferry ride can take anywhere from 30 minutes to 5 hours, with many islands offering direct routes.

For instance, Santorini, one of the most popular destinations in the Cyclades, is about 4-5 hours by ferry from Piraeus. If you're heading to Mykonos, the ferry ride typically takes around 2.5 to 3 hours. The faster ferries, such as the high-speed catamarans, can get you to your destination in a fraction of the time, while the slower conventional ferries offer a more leisurely journey with the chance to enjoy the sea breeze and stunning views as you approach the islands.

Ferries in Greece are generally reliable, but it's always a good idea to book your tickets in advance, especially if you're traveling during peak tourist season (June to September). You can easily book tickets online through websites like Ferryhopper or directly at the port. Some ferry operators even offer flexible tickets, which allow you to change your departure date if your plans shift.

By Plane: Quick and Convenient

If you're short on time or simply prefer a faster option, flying is another great way to get to the Cyclades. Several of the islands, including Santorini, Mykonos, Naxos, and Paros, have airports that are connected to Athens International Airport (Eleftherios Venizelos). Flights to these islands are relatively short, typically ranging from 30 minutes to 1 hour, and there are frequent flights during the high season.

Flying can be a bit pricier than taking the ferry, but if you're in a rush or just prefer to minimize travel time, it's an excellent choice. Once you arrive, most airports are a short distance from the main towns or ports, so you'll be able to dive into your island adventure in no time.

Island Hopping: Connecting the Dots Between Islands

One of the highlights of traveling in the Cyclades is island hopping—visiting multiple islands on the same trip. Since the Cyclades are so well connected, you can easily travel from one island to the next by ferry. From Mykonos, you can hop over to

Delos, a sacred island with ancient ruins. From Santorini, you can make your way to Milos, with its stunning beaches and volcanic formations, or to Ios, known for its lively atmosphere.

There are multiple ferry companies operating throughout the Cyclades, so you can plan your journey based on the islands you want to visit. Ferryhopper offers a "hop on, hop off" style of booking that allows you to buy a multi-leg ticket for traveling between islands, which is perfect for an extended trip. Alternatively, you can also charter a private boat for a more intimate and personalized island-hopping experience, although this is a more expensive option.

When planning your island-hopping journey, be mindful of ferry schedules, as they can vary depending on the season and weather conditions. The summer months (June to September) tend to have the most frequent connections between islands, while the winter months may have fewer routes. It's advisable to check schedules ahead of time and be flexible with your plans in case of changes.

Traveling Between Islands: Tips for Smooth Sailing

- *Book in Advance:* Especially during high season, ferries can fill up quickly. Booking your tickets ahead of time ensures a stress-free experience and helps you avoid the disappointment of a full ferry.
- *Pack Light:* Since you'll be hopping from island to island, it's best to pack light. Many ferries have limited storage space, and having fewer bags means easier travel and more freedom.
- *Check for Delays:* While ferry travel is generally reliable, weather conditions (especially in the off-season) can

sometimes cause delays. Always double-check ferry departure times and give yourself some flexibility in your schedule.

- Boat Tours for Hidden Gems: If you have extra time, consider taking a boat tour to explore hidden coves, secluded beaches, or nearby islands that aren't easily accessible by ferry.

Whether you choose the scenic ferry ride or the quick flight, the Cyclades islands are incredibly accessible from Athens, making it easy to tailor your travel experience to your preferences.

10 Fascinating Facts

1. A Group of Islands in the Aegean Sea

The Cyclades is an archipelago of 220 islands located in the Aegean Sea. However, only around 30 of these islands are inhabited, each offering a unique cultural and natural experience.

2. The Name "Cyclades"

The name "Cyclades" comes from the Greek word "kyklos", meaning "circle." The islands are named this way because they form a circular shape around the sacred island of Delos, an important archaeological site in Greek history.

3. Home to the Ancient Minoan Civilization

Several islands in the Cyclades, including Santorini and Kea, were once home to the Minoan civilization, which flourished around 2000–1400 BCE. Santorini's volcanic eruption around 1600 BCE is believed to have contributed to the end of the Minoan civilization.

4. Famous for Its Unique Architecture

The islands are renowned for their traditional Cycladic architecture—whitewashed houses with blue domes, narrow streets, and colorful doorways. This style is designed to reflect the sun and keep homes cool during the hot summer months.

5. Santorini's Volcano

Santorini is home to an active volcano that erupted catastrophically in ancient times, leading to the creation of the island's distinctive caldera. The eruption is also thought to have inspired the legend of Atlantis.

6. Milos is a Miner's Paradise

Milos was historically known for its mining industry, and the island is still home to significant volcanic minerals and mineral deposits. It was once a major source of obsidian and sulfur in ancient Greece.

7. Mykonos is Known for Its Nightlife

While the Cyclades are famous for their natural beauty and historical significance, Mykonos stands out for its vibrant nightlife. The island is a party destination, drawing international visitors for its beach clubs, bars, and night parties.

8. Delos: The Birthplace of Apollo and Artemis

The island of Delos, now a UNESCO World Heritage Site, is considered one of the most important archaeological sites in Greece. According to Greek mythology, Apollo and Artemis were born on Delos, making the island a sacred place in antiquity.

9. Ios is a Haven for Hikers

Ios is not only known for its beautiful beaches but also for its hiking trails. The island offers several scenic paths, including the famous trail leading to the St. John's Monastery with panoramic views of the Aegean.

10. Windmills of Mykonos

The windmills of Mykonos are an iconic symbol of the island. These 15th-century windmills, once used for milling grain, are now one of the most photographed landmarks in the Cyclades and offer spectacular views of the harbor and sunsets.

Chapter 1
Santorini – The Island of Dreams

Mesmerizing Sunsets at Oia

Santorini's sunsets are the stuff of legend, and there's no better place to witness this natural spectacle than in the iconic village of **Oia**. As the sun dips below the horizon, it paints the sky with hues of vibrant oranges, pinks, and purples, creating a breathtaking scene that leaves visitors in awe. The whole village seems to glow as the golden light reflects off the caldera and the whitewashed buildings, casting a surreal and almost magical ambiance.

Oia has become synonymous with sunset views, and it's easy to see why. The narrow streets of the village wind their way towards the famous viewpoint, where crowds gather hours before sunset to secure their spot. It's not just about watching the sun set; it's the collective hush that falls over the crowd as everyone becomes entranced by the beauty unfolding before them.

For an even more magical experience, head to the **Oia Castle Ruins**. While this spot can get crowded, the view of the sun setting behind the caldera and the nearby islands is unparalleled. As the sun begins to set, the sky reflects off the water, creating a kaleidoscope of colors that dance on the surface. It's the perfect moment to capture that postcard-worthy photo—or better yet, to simply soak it all in and relish in the beauty of nature.

If you want to escape the crowds, there are plenty of quieter spots around Oia, such as cafes with a view or tucked-away terraces where you can sip a drink and watch the sky transform. Whether you're traveling with a loved one, friends, or solo, Santorini's sunsets are an experience that stays with you long after you've left the island.

Discovering the Black Sand Beaches

Santorini's beaches are as unique as the island itself, shaped by the island's volcanic history. The striking **black sand beaches** are one of the island's most distinctive features, with their rich, dark sand providing a striking contrast against the clear blue waters of the Aegean Sea. These beaches are the result of volcanic lava, which over centuries has formed soft, fine, black sands that are warm underfoot, adding to the allure of the island's coastal charm.

Kamari Beach is one of the most famous black sand beaches on Santorini, and it's the perfect spot to spend a lazy day by the sea. The beach is lined with a long promenade filled with restaurants, cafes, and shops, making it ideal for those who enjoy a bit of hustle and bustle alongside their beach day. The crystal-clear waters here are perfect for swimming, and there are plenty of sunbeds and umbrellas to rent for a relaxing day in the sun. Kamari is also great for families, with calm waters that make it safe for young swimmers.

Just a short distance away is **Perissa Beach**, another black sand haven. Perissa is quieter than Kamari but offers a laid-back, peaceful vibe. The beach stretches for miles, offering plenty of space to spread out and enjoy the sun in relative peace. For the more adventurous, **Perissa** is ideal for water sports such as windsurfing or paddleboarding. There's also a selection of seaside tavernas where you can enjoy freshly caught seafood and traditional Greek dishes while gazing out over the shimmering waters.

If you're seeking a more secluded experience, **Red Beach** offers a dramatic setting with its red-tinted cliffs rising above the black sand shore. This beach is located near the village of Akrotiri, and though it's one of the more famous beaches on the island, its natural beauty makes it worth the visit. The combination of red volcanic cliffs and dark sands creates a striking contrast against the blue sea, making it a perfect location for photographers. While the beach can get crowded during peak season, early mornings or later in the evening offer a peaceful, almost private atmosphere.

For those seeking even more tranquility, consider **Vlychada Beach** on the southern coast of Santorini. The beach is framed by towering white cliffs that have been sculpted by the wind and water, creating an almost lunar landscape. The beach itself is quieter, with fewer tourists, making it a fantastic spot for a peaceful swim or sunbathing. There's a small marina nearby, and the beach is less commercialized, offering a more natural experience. Vlychada is also known for its clear waters, making it a favorite for snorkeling enthusiasts.

Santorini's volcanic beaches are perfect for those who want to explore the island's rugged beauty while enjoying a day at the sea. The warm black sand and the crystal-clear waters provide a refreshing contrast to the stunning, arid landscape that defines the island. Whether you want to relax, enjoy water sports, or simply take in the stunning views, Santorini's black sand beaches will captivate you in their own unique way.

Exploring Ancient Akrotiri: A Window into the Past

Santorini isn't just a visual feast of sun-kissed beaches and whitewashed buildings; it's also a treasure trove of history that dates back thousands of years. One of the most significant archaeological sites in the Cyclades, **Akrotiri**, offers visitors a rare and fascinating glimpse into the ancient world. Known as the "Minoan Pompeii," this ancient city was buried under layers of volcanic ash after a catastrophic eruption around 1600 BCE, preserving much of the city in an incredible state of preservation.

As you step onto the site, you're walking on the ground of a thriving Bronze Age settlement that was once home to a sophisticated civilization. The eruption, though devastating for the inhabitants of Akrotiri, became the very reason why the city is so well preserved. The volcanic ash, while burying the city, also protected it from the elements, leaving behind intricate frescoes, multi-story buildings, and even everyday items like pottery and furniture—giving us an unprecedented look at the lives of the island's ancient inhabitants.

A Walk Through the Ruins: Ancient Streets and Buildings

One of the first things you'll notice as you wander through Akrotiri is how advanced the city was for its time. The architecture is a mix of large, multi-story buildings that were connected by narrow streets, much like the modern cities we live in today. The buildings were made with thick walls that helped to protect the inhabitants from the heat and earthquakes, showcasing the engineering ingenuity of the Minoans.

As you walk along the preserved streets, you can imagine what life might have been like in this ancient city. The layout is surprisingly organized, with clear divisions of residential, commercial, and public spaces. You can peer into the remnants of homes that were once filled with the sounds of daily life—kitchens, living spaces, and storage areas. Some homes had even been decorated with beautiful **frescoes** depicting vibrant scenes of nature, animals, and life on the island, giving a glimpse into the art and culture of the time.

The streets themselves are remarkably well preserved, and it's possible to follow the original pathways, flanked by ancient walls, as you explore the area. You'll encounter places where the remains of ancient pottery and tools have been uncovered, adding another layer of understanding about the daily life of the people who lived here. Akrotiri was clearly a center of trade and culture, with evidence of its residents' advanced knowledge of architecture, art, and trade networks.

The Frescoes: A Window into the Past

Perhaps the most striking feature of Akrotiri is its **frescoes**—paintings that adorned the walls of private homes, public buildings, and temples. These ancient works of art are some of the best-preserved examples of Minoan frescoes in the world. They depict scenes of vibrant life on the island, showcasing lush landscapes, bustling markets, and rituals, as well as marine life like dolphins and fish.

One of the most famous frescoes from Akrotiri is the **"Spring Fresco"**, which depicts a lively scene of flowers and birds. The colors are incredibly vivid, even after thousands of years, and provide an incredible insight into the natural world and the artistic style of the Minoan civilization. Other frescoes feature images of daily life, such as traders at markets and scenes of processions, offering a glimpse into the religious practices and cultural values of the time.

The frescoes are thought to have had a dual purpose: not only were they decorative, but they also served as a way to communicate cultural identity, religious beliefs, and the prosperity of the community. As you gaze upon these ancient works, it's easy to feel connected to the past, as though you're standing in the very same spaces where people once gathered to admire the art and beauty around them.

The Eruption and Its Legacy

The eruption of Santorini's volcano, known as the **Minoan eruption**, is one of the most significant volcanic events in recorded history. The eruption was so powerful that it caused massive devastation, not only to Akrotiri but to surrounding regions as well, including Crete. The ash and pumice that buried Akrotiri preserved the city, much like the way Pompeii was preserved by the eruption of Mount Vesuvius. However, unlike Pompeii, which was preserved by ash falling on the city, Akrotiri was buried by a massive blanket of pumice and ash, which allowed for an even better level of preservation.

The eruption likely led to the collapse of the Minoan civilization, as it disrupted trade routes and caused agricultural destruction. The volcanic event is also thought to have contributed to the eventual decline of the ancient city, which had been a thriving hub of culture and commerce. Yet, despite this catastrophe, the legacy of Akrotiri lives on, offering a snapshot of what life was like in one of the Aegean's most sophisticated and prosperous ancient cities.

The museum in **Fira** houses many of the artifacts discovered at the site, including pottery, jewelry, and statues, offering additional context and helping to bring the ancient city to life. Visiting Akrotiri is like stepping back in time, and it's easy to feel like a time traveler as you explore the site and imagine the lives of the people who once lived there.

Where to Eat, Stay, and Play: Insider Tips

Santorini is a dream destination not just for its stunning landscapes but also for its rich culinary offerings, luxurious stays, and an array of activities. Whether you're a foodie, culture lover, beachgoer, or adventurer, Santorini has something for everyone. Here's a comprehensive guide to help you make the most of your time on the island, from where to eat to the best places to stay and activities you can't miss.

Where to Eat: Culinary Delights of Santorini

Santorini's food scene is a reflection of the island's rich history and unique volcanic soil. From fine dining to casual street food, here are some of the best places to eat.

Selene Restaurant (Pyrgos)

Located in the charming village of Pyrgos, **Selene** is one of Santorini's most renowned restaurants, perfect for those who want to experience high-end Greek cuisine with a modern twist. Known for its innovative approach to traditional dishes, Selene offers a seasonal menu with local ingredients like fresh fish, organic vegetables, and unique herbs.

- **Price Range**: €50–€90 per person (excluding drinks)

- **Distance**: Pyrgos is about 10 km from Fira (15–20 minutes by car)
- **Specialty**: Santorini fava (yellow split pea dip) and their signature wine pairings.

Taverna Katina (Amoudi Bay)

Tucked at the base of Oia, **Taverna Katina** offers some of the freshest seafood on the island. Sitting right by the water at Amoudi Bay, it's the perfect spot to enjoy your meal while watching the fisherman haul in their fresh catch. The **grilled octopus** and **seafood pasta** are highly recommended.

- **Price Range**: €25–€40 per person (for a seafood meal)
- **Distance**: Amoudi Bay is around 2.5 km from Oia (5 minutes by car)
- **Specialty**: Fresh fish, grilled octopus, and seafood platters.

Lucky's Souvlakis (Fira)

If you're looking for a quick, affordable meal that doesn't compromise on taste, **Lucky's Souvlakis** in Fira is the place to go. Known for its excellent souvlaki (grilled meat skewers), this family-run eatery serves one of the best fast casual bites on the island. The pork or chicken souvlaki wraps are flavorful and filling.

- **Price Range**: €5–€8 per person
- **Distance**: Located in Fira, just a short walk from the main square.
- **Specialty**: Pork souvlaki wraps and Greek salads.

Ammoudi Fish Tavern (Oia)

In Amoudi Bay, Ammoudi Fish Tavern offers a fantastic view and great seafood. With a front-row seat to the sea, you can savor freshly prepared dishes, including sea bream, grilled lobster, and shrimp saganaki.

- **Price Range**: €30–€50 per person (depending on the seafood you choose)
- **Distance**: About 2.5 km from Oia (5 minutes by car)
- **Specialty**: Freshly caught fish and shrimp saganaki.

Katerina's Restaurant (Oia)

A more casual but equally delightful option, **Katerina's Restaurant** in Oia offers fantastic Greek fare, including **moussaka** and **souvlaki**. Its terrace offers fantastic sunset views, making it the perfect place to enjoy a relaxed meal after a long day of sightseeing.

- **Price Range**: €20–€35 per person
- **Distance**: Situated in Oia's central square.
- **Specialty**: Moussaka and grilled meats.

Where to Stay: Unique Accommodations in Santorini

Santorini offers a diverse range of accommodations, from luxury cliffside resorts with infinity pools to charming boutique hotels. Below are some of the best places to stay depending on your budget and preferences:

Katikies Hotel (Oia)

For a once-in-a-lifetime experience, stay at **Katikies Hotel** in Oia. Known for its stunning whitewashed architecture, breathtaking views of the caldera, and incredible service, Katikies is the epitome of luxury in Santorini. The hotel features cave-style suites, many with private balconies and plunge pools.

- **Price Range**: €400–€1,000+ per night (depending on the suite)
- **Distance**: Located in Oia, about a 10-minute walk from the Oia Castle viewpoint.
- **Specialty**: Private plunge pools, panoramic caldera views, and sunset vistas.

Canaves Oia Suites & Spa (Oia)

For those seeking a more secluded yet equally luxurious experience, **Canaves Oia Suites & Spa** offers stunning cave-style suites with private terraces and hot tubs overlooking the caldera. It also features a world-class spa for those looking to relax after a day of exploring.

- **Price Range**: €500–€1,200 per night
- **Distance**: Located in the heart of Oia.
- **Specialty**: Infinity pools, cave-style suites, and a luxury spa.

Astra Suites (Imerovigli)

Located in the quieter town of **Imerovigli**, **Astra Suites** offers incredible views of the caldera without the crowds of Oia. The suites are spacious and feature private balconies, hot tubs, and stunning vistas. This boutique hotel is ideal for couples seeking romance and peace.

- **Price Range**: €300–€800 per night
- **Distance**: Approximately 2 km from Fira.
- **Specialty**: Intimate atmosphere, luxurious cave suites, and panoramic views.

Hotel Sunny Villas (Imerovigli)

If you're looking for a more affordable option with luxurious touches, **Hotel Sunny Villas** offers great value. Located in Imerovigli, it features stunning cliff-side views, a lovely pool, and charming, comfortable rooms. It's a perfect base for couples and those wanting to avoid the crowds.

- **Price Range**: €150–€300 per night
- **Distance**: 2 km from Fira, accessible by a short car ride.
- **Specialty**: Friendly service, cozy ambiance, and amazing sunset views.

Astra Suites (Imerovigli)

For a tranquil, romantic stay, **Astra Suites** in Imerovigli offers spacious, luxury suites with spectacular views of the caldera. It's perfect for those seeking privacy and luxury.

- **Price Range**: €300–€600 per night
- **Distance**: About 2 km from Fira.
- **Specialty**: Quiet atmosphere, cave suites, caldera views.

Where to Play: Activities and Adventures

Santorini is more than just beaches and sunsets. From thrilling water sports to unique cultural experiences, here are some activities that will make your visit unforgettable:

Boat Tours and Sailing Around the Caldera

The caldera is the heart of Santorini, and the best way to explore it is by boat. Many tour operators offer half-day and full-day **sailing tours**, which include stops at volcanic islands like **Nea Kameni** and **Palia Kameni**, where you can take a dip in hot springs. Some tours even offer wine tasting on board or the chance to swim at secluded beaches.

- **Price Range**: €50–€150 per person for a group tour, private charters starting at €500.
- **Duration**: 4–6 hours for most tours.
- **Specialty**: Volcanic hot springs, snorkeling, and wine tasting on board.

Hiking from Fira to Oia

The hike from **Fira** to **Oia** is one of Santorini's most famous outdoor activities, and it's easy to see why. The 10-kilometer trek takes you along the caldera's edge, offering panoramic views of the island's cliffs and sparkling waters. It's a moderate hike that can be completed in about 3-4 hours, depending on your pace.

- **Distance**: 10 km (6 miles).
- **Duration**: 3-4 hours.
- **Difficulty**: Moderate.

- **Specialty**: Spectacular views, passing through small villages and vineyards.

Wine Tasting and Vineyard Tours

Santorini is known for its unique **Assyrtiko wine**, made from grapes grown in the volcanic soil. Take a tour of local wineries like **Santo Wines** and **Venetsanos Winery** to taste some of the island's best wines while enjoying sweeping views of the caldera. Most wineries offer guided tours that explain the wine-making process, followed by a tasting session.

- **Price Range**: €30–€80 per person for a wine-tasting tour.
- **Duration**: 2–3 hours.
- **Specialty**: Assyrtiko wine, volcanic soil, sunset views.

Cultural and Historical Tours

Santorini is steeped in history, and a visit to **Akrotiri**—the ancient Minoan city preserved by volcanic ash—is a must. Explore this fascinating archaeological site to see ancient frescoes, preserved buildings, and the incredible engineering feats of the Minoan civilization. For a deeper dive into the island's history, visit the **Museum of Prehistoric Thira** in Fira.

- **Price Range**: €10–€20 for entry to Akrotiri or museums.
- **Duration**: 1–2 hours at each site.
- **Specialty**: Ancient Minoan civilization, volcanic history.

Image by AXP Photography on Unsplash

Chapter 2

Mykonos – A Glimpse of Glamour

Wandering the Maze of Mykonos Town

Mykonos Town, also known as **Chora**, is a place where the past and present collide in the most enchanting way. As you stroll through the narrow, winding streets of this charming town, it feels like you're stepping into a living postcard. The town is a labyrinth of whitewashed buildings, charming bougainvillea-covered walls, and cobblestone streets that twist and turn, leading you to discover new gems at every corner. The maze-like layout of the town was originally designed to confuse pirates, and today, it serves as the perfect place for visitors to get lost and uncover the true essence of Mykonos.

The town's architecture is a beautiful blend of traditional Cycladic style with touches of Venetian influence, as Mykonos has long been a crossroads of cultures. Whitewashed walls with blue shutters, red domed churches, and colorful doors create a picturesque setting that's a photographer's dream. The streets are dotted with small, family-owned shops selling handcrafted goods, jewelry, local art, and colorful textiles—perfect for picking up a unique souvenir or gift.

Image by Nella N on Unsplash

Matoyianni Street is the heart of Mykonos Town, bustling with life throughout the day. This pedestrianized street is lined with high-end boutiques, international designer stores, and trendy cafes. Whether you're looking for a stylish new outfit or simply want to enjoy a coffee while people-watching, this street has something for everyone. As you wander further, you'll stumble upon hidden corners, quiet squares, and charming tavernas where locals and visitors mingle in a relaxed atmosphere.

One of the best ways to experience Mykonos Town is on foot. The winding streets lead you to hidden gems like the **Tria Pigadia** (Three Wells), a charming little square with three ancient wells that date back to the island's early history. Another must-see is the **Kato Mili Windmills**, which sit high above the town, offering panoramic views of the island and the sparkling Aegean Sea. These iconic windmills are a reminder of the island's maritime heritage and provide the perfect spot to stop and take in the breathtaking views.

As evening falls, Mykonos Town takes on a completely different vibe. The narrow streets are illuminated by warm golden lights, and the air is filled with the sounds of clinking glasses, lively chatter, and soft music. The town transforms into a romantic setting, perfect for an evening stroll before dinner or a drink at one of the many rooftop bars with a view of the caldera.

The Iconic Windmills and Little Venice

The **windmills of Mykonos** are undoubtedly one of the island's most iconic features. These towering white structures, standing proudly against the deep blue sky, offer not only a glimpse into the island's past but also some of the best panoramic views of the town and the surrounding sea. The windmills were built in the 16th century and were once used to grind wheat, taking advantage of the strong Aegean winds that sweep across the island. Today, only a few of these windmills remain, but they stand as an important historical symbol of Mykonos' agrarian past.

The most famous of these windmills are located above **Mykonos Town** in the **Kato Mili** area. These picturesque structures are often seen in photographs and postcards, their large, white sails reaching high above the town. Visiting the windmills is a must-do for anyone on the island, as the view from this elevated spot is simply breathtaking. From here, you can see **Mykonos Town** spread out beneath you, the Aegean Sea stretching into the horizon, and, on clear days, nearby islands like **Delos**.

While some of the windmills are still in operation today, many have been repurposed into small museums or private homes. At sunset, the windmills are especially magical. The golden light of the setting sun casts long shadows, making the windmills look almost ethereal as the sky turns a soft pink and orange. This is one of the most photographed spots on the island, so be sure to capture the moment.

Just below the windmills, you'll find **Little Venice**, one of the most charming and picturesque districts in Mykonos Town. This area, which is named after the famous Venetian-inspired architecture, is made up of colorful buildings that seem to spill directly into the sea. Many of the buildings in Little Venice were originally merchant houses, but today they house trendy bars, restaurants, and cafes that offer stunning views of the water.

The appeal of Little Venice lies not only in its architecture but in its unique setting. The sea laps at the foundations of the buildings, and at sunset, the view of the sky changing colors over the water creates a magical atmosphere. As you walk through Little Venice, the sights, sounds, and smells come together to create an unforgettable experience. You'll hear the gentle lapping of the waves against the stone walls, the chatter of people dining al fresco, and the occasional clink of glasses as locals and tourists alike gather to enjoy their evening.

For a true experience of Little Venice, stop by one of the cafes or bars and enjoy a cocktail while watching the sunset. The area is known for its lively nightlife, and the bars here often feature live music or DJ sets. Some of the most famous bars in Little Venice include **Caprice Bar**, which is perfect for enjoying a drink while watching the sunset, and **Katerina's Bar**, a more laid-back spot offering cocktails and a relaxed atmosphere.

Little Venice is a place where the past and present coexist in harmony, with the stunning architecture offering a glimpse into Mykonos' Venetian history, and the vibrant nightlife providing a modern, lively twist.

A Nightlife Like No Other: Bars, Clubs, and Beach Parties

Mykonos is famous around the world for its **vibrant nightlife**, and it's no exaggeration to say that the island comes alive after sunset in a way few other destinations can match. From beachfront parties that continue into the early hours of the morning to upscale nightclubs that draw international DJs, Mykonos offers a wide variety of options for those looking to dance, drink, and socialize under the stars. Whether you're a party enthusiast or just someone looking to enjoy a cocktail while watching the sunset, Mykonos' nightlife scene has something for everyone.

Cavo Paradiso is one of the most iconic nightclubs on the island, perched high above **Paradise Beach**. This open-air club is known for its spectacular views of the sea, the stars above, and the breathtaking surroundings. With a dance floor that seems to stretch into the horizon, Cavo Paradiso has hosted some of the biggest names in electronic music, from Tiësto to David Guetta. The sound system is state-of-the-art, and the atmosphere is electric, with revelers dancing to world-class DJs until dawn.

- **Price Range**: €20–€50 for entry (sometimes more for big events), drinks €10–€20.
- **Distance**: 6 km from Mykonos Town (15 minutes by car).
- **Specialty**: International DJs, stunning sea views, unforgettable atmosphere.

Another hotspot for the party crowd is **Scorpios Mykonos**, located at **Paraga Beach**. Scorpios offers a slightly different vibe from the frenetic energy of Cavo Paradiso. It's part beach club, part bohemian retreat, with a laid-back atmosphere that gradually intensifies as the day turns into night. By day, it's a chic spot to relax by the sea, enjoying organic food and handcrafted cocktails. By night, however, Scorpios transforms into one of the island's most exclusive venues, with live music performances, immersive experiences, and top-tier DJs. The sunset views here are particularly stunning, making it the ideal spot to watch the sky change color before the beats drop.

- **Price Range**: Entry €20–€50, drinks €15–€25.

- **Distance**: 7 km from Mykonos Town (15 minutes by car).
- **Specialty**: Bohemian-chic atmosphere, live performances, sunset parties.

For those seeking a more relaxed yet stylish experience, Alemagou Beach Club on Ftelia Beach is an excellent choice. This venue is known for its laid-back vibes, chilled-out music, and beautiful setting. Alemagou is less about big-name DJs and more about enjoying the sounds of the sea and the breeze while sipping cocktails and socializing with fellow travelers. It's the perfect spot to unwind and mingle in a beautiful, tranquil setting while still enjoying the lively Mykonos energy.

- **Price Range**: €30–€50 for sunbeds, cocktails €12–€20.
- **Distance**: 9 km from Mykonos Town (20 minutes by car).
- **Specialty**: Relaxed atmosphere, laid-back beach vibes, great for sunset views.

If you prefer a more intimate bar scene, head to Mykonos Town, where you'll find plenty of bars offering cocktails, wine, and craft drinks. Caprice Bar in Little Venice is one of the most popular spots, offering not only great drinks but also a front-row seat to Mykonos' famous sunsets. The bar overlooks the Aegean Sea, and it's a perfect spot to enjoy an Aperol spritz or a glass of wine as you watch the sun dip below the horizon.

- **Price Range**: €10–€20 for drinks.
- **Distance**: Located in Little Venice, Mykonos Town.
- **Specialty**: Stunning sunset views, cocktails by the sea.

Jackie O' Beach Club & Restaurant is another standout, located in the beautiful **Super Paradise Beach** area. This iconic beach club has become one of Mykonos' most inclusive and glamorous spots, with an eclectic crowd drawn to its elegant poolside and beachside bars. Whether you're here to enjoy a relaxed afternoon or dance the night away to house music, Jackie O' offers an upscale yet friendly environment. The crowd is a mix of LGBTQ+ travelers and others looking for an extravagant and unforgettable experience.

- **Price Range**: Entry free for most events, drinks €15–€25.
- **Distance**: 6 km from Mykonos Town (15 minutes by car).
- **Specialty**: Inclusive vibe, upscale beach club, drag shows.

For those who prefer something a bit more intimate, Katerina's Bar in Mykonos Town offers a friendly and cozy atmosphere. Located in Little Venice, the bar has a great selection of drinks and is known for its lively, welcoming atmosphere. Whether you're there for a quiet evening drink or to mingle with locals and fellow travelers, Katerina's provides a more relaxed way to enjoy Mykonos nightlife without the intensity of some of the bigger clubs.

- **Price Range**: €8–€15 for drinks.
- **Distance**: Located in Little Venice, Mykonos Town.
- **Specialty**: Casual drinks, cozy atmosphere, great for mingling.

Relaxing Beach Vibes: Psarou, Paradise, and Beyond

While Mykonos is renowned for its lively party scene, it also offers several idyllic beaches where you can unwind and enjoy the serene beauty of the Aegean Sea. Whether you're looking to relax in style, swim in crystal-clear waters, or escape the crowds, Mykonos' beaches have something for everyone. Here are some of the best beaches for those seeking a more peaceful, laid-back experience.

Psarou Beach: Exclusive and Chic

Psarou Beach is one of Mykonos' most exclusive and fashionable beaches, attracting a chic crowd looking for a luxurious, sophisticated experience. The beach is lined with high-end beach clubs, and it's not uncommon to spot a celebrity lounging on one of its plush sunbeds. The crystal-clear waters are perfect for swimming, while the soft golden sand provides an ideal place to bask under the Mediterranean sun.

At **Nammos Beach Club**, one of the most famous spots on the island, guests can enjoy top-tier service, gourmet food, and refreshing cocktails. Nammos is known for its laid-back yet upscale vibe, where you can enjoy a stylish afternoon by the sea or dance to live music as the sun sets. Whether you're lounging by the beach or enjoying a meal, Psarou offers the perfect balance of exclusivity and relaxation.

- **Price Range**: Sunbeds €50–€150 (depending on location); drinks €15–€30.

- **Distance**: 5 km from Mykonos Town (10 minutes by car).

- **Specialty**: Upscale beach club, crystal-clear waters, celebrity sightings.

Paradise Beach: Iconic Beach Parties with a Laid-Back Vibe

While **Paradise Beach** is known for its vibrant party scene, it also offers plenty of opportunities for relaxation during the day. The beach itself has soft golden sand, shallow waters, and plenty of space to stretch out and enjoy the sunshine. While the beach gets more lively in the afternoon with music and beach parties, early mornings and late evenings offer a quieter atmosphere perfect for swimming or simply unwinding.

The beach is home to several beach bars and restaurants where you can enjoy casual Greek meals, fresh seafood, and refreshing drinks. Paradise Beach Club and Tropicana Beach Bar are popular venues for those looking for a more laid-back beach day before the party atmosphere takes over. For a more peaceful experience, find a quieter corner of the beach and enjoy the sun in peace while watching the waves crash on the shore.

- **Price Range**: Free entry, sunbeds €20–€50; drinks €10–€20.
- **Distance**: 6 km from Mykonos Town (15 minutes by car).
- **Specialty**: Perfect mix of relaxation and fun, beachfront dining, calm mornings and evenings.

Agios Sostis Beach: Tranquil and Untouched

For those who are seeking **seclusion** and tranquility, **Agios Sostis Beach** is a hidden gem on the northern side of the island. Unlike some of the more tourist-heavy beaches, Agios Sostis has remained relatively untouched, offering a more serene and natural environment. The beach is long and quiet, with golden sand and beautiful clear waters, perfect for those who prefer peace over the party scene.

The beach is not fully developed, so there are no beach clubs or bars here, which only adds to its charm. If you want to grab a drink or snack, head to the nearby **Kiki's Tavern**, a family-run restaurant that serves delicious homemade Greek food in a beautiful, rustic setting. Enjoy a leisurely lunch in the shaded outdoor area while watching the waves lap against the shore.

- **Price Range**: Free entry; Kiki's Tavern meals €10–€25.
- **Distance**: 8 km from Mykonos Town (20 minutes by car).
- **Specialty**: Quiet, untouched beauty, no crowds, family-run tavernas.

Elia Beach: Relaxation and Watersports Combined

Elia Beach is one of the largest beaches on Mykonos, offering plenty of space for both relaxation and water activities. The beach is less crowded than some of the island's other popular beaches, making it perfect for those who want to soak up the sun without the noise. The golden sand is soft underfoot, and the turquoise waters are perfect for swimming and snorkeling.

Elia Beach has a selection of beach bars and restaurants where you can enjoy refreshing drinks and delicious meals. The **Elia Beach Club** offers sunbeds and umbrellas, along with great food and music in the background. If you're into water sports, you can also rent equipment for activities such as jet skiing, paddleboarding, and windsurfing. It's the perfect beach to combine relaxation with a little adventure.

- **Price Range**: Sunbeds €30–€60; drinks €10–€20.
- **Distance**: 10 km from Mykonos Town (20 minutes by car).
- **Specialty**: Spacious beach, watersports, and a peaceful atmosphere.

Agios Ioannis: A Quiet Retreat with Stunning Views

Agios Ioannis is one of the most peaceful and beautiful beaches on Mykonos, located on the southern side of the island. The beach is quieter than other areas like Paradise or Psarou, making it ideal for those looking to unwind and enjoy some peace and quiet. The sand is soft and golden, and the water is shallow, making it perfect for families or anyone who enjoys swimming in calm waters.

The beach is lined with a few low-key restaurants and beach clubs, where you can enjoy a leisurely meal or sip on a cocktail while watching the waves. The views from Agios Ioannis are simply spectacular—across the bay, you'll see **Delos Island**, an archaeological site that is one of Greece's most important ancient ruins. This backdrop adds a sense of serenity to the entire experience, making it a perfect spot for a quiet afternoon.

- **Price Range**: Free entry; sunbeds €20–€40; drinks €8–€15.
- **Distance**: 4 km from Mykonos Town (10 minutes by car).
- **Specialty**: Tranquil beach, views of Delos Island, ideal for families and peaceful afternoons.

Chapter 3
Paros – Serenity in Simplicity

Image by Despina Galani on Unsplash

The Charm of Naoussa and Parikia

Paros, often overlooked in favor of its more famous neighbors like Mykonos and Santorini, is a true gem in the Cyclades, offering a peaceful and authentic experience. Two of the island's most enchanting towns, Naoussa and Parikia, capture the essence of Paros, each with its own charm and atmosphere.

Naoussa, on the northern tip of the island, is a picturesque fishing village that has managed to retain its traditional charm while embracing modern comforts. The village is built around a small harbor where local fishermen dock their boats, giving Naoussa a peaceful, maritime feel. The town's winding streets are lined with whitewashed houses, boutique shops, art galleries, and cafés, making it the perfect place to get lost in the quiet beauty of island life.

As you stroll along the harbor, you'll encounter numerous seafood tavernas serving freshly caught fish, where you can enjoy a leisurely meal by the water. The old Venetian port is especially charming at sunset when the sky turns golden and the reflection of the boats and buildings shimmer on the surface of the water. For those seeking a lively atmosphere, Naoussa has a vibrant nightlife scene, with trendy bars and nightclubs offering everything from relaxed cocktails to upbeat dance music, often set against a backdrop of the Aegean Sea.

On the other hand, Parikia, the island's capital, offers a more laid-back, yet equally captivating experience. Parikia is known for its traditional Cycladic architecture, with narrow streets lined with whitewashed houses, blue shutters, and bougainvillea-covered walls. As the ferry port of Paros, it is the first point of entry for most visitors, but it's much more than just a transport hub. The town is home to several historic sites, including the impressive Church of Panagia Ekatontapiliani, one of the oldest and most important churches in Greece.

The atmosphere in Parikia is more relaxed than Naoussa, and you'll find plenty of quiet spots to enjoy a coffee or a light meal while soaking in the surrounding beauty. The town's waterfront promenade is a lovely place to walk in the evening, offering stunning views of the Aegean and the neighboring islands. You'll also find a selection of local boutiques, selling handcrafted jewelry, textiles, and artisanal products, perfect for picking up a unique souvenir.

Both towns offer a glimpse into authentic island life, with their quaint streets, historic charm, and stunning sea views, making them the perfect bases to explore the rest of Paros.

Hidden Beaches and Crystal-Clear Waters

Paros is a haven for those seeking a more serene and untouched beach experience. While the island is known for its popular beaches like Golden Beach and Santa Maria, there are many lesser-known coves and shores that offer an escape from the crowds. These hidden beaches, with their crystal-clear waters and peaceful atmosphere, provide the perfect environment for those who prefer quiet, secluded spots to relax and enjoy the natural beauty of the island.

One of the most hidden gems on the island is Kolymbithres Beach, located in the Paros Park area, on the northern side of the island. What makes this beach unique is its striking landscape—large granite rocks have been smoothed by centuries of wind and water, creating shallow pools that are perfect for swimming. The beach itself is protected by the rocks, giving it a calm, sheltered atmosphere. Kolymbithres is perfect for those who want to relax and sunbathe without the noise and hustle of more crowded beaches. The clear waters are ideal for swimming or kayaking, and there's a peaceful vibe that makes it a perfect place to escape.

Not far from Kolymbithres, you'll find Monastiri Beach, a quieter spot that's often overlooked by tourists. This small, sandy beach is surrounded by natural beauty, including fragrant pine trees and lush vegetation. The shallow waters are calm and clear, making it ideal for families or anyone looking to enjoy a peaceful swim. Monastiri Beach also has a small beach bar, where you can grab a cold drink and some light snacks while enjoying the view.

Agia Irini Beach, located just outside of Parikia, is another serene spot worth exploring. This beach has a more relaxed and local feel, with just a few tavernas offering traditional Greek food. The clear waters here are perfect for swimming, and the beach is often less crowded, making it an excellent choice for those seeking solitude. Agia Irini is a great place to spend an afternoon enjoying the simplicity of the surroundings—clear waters, soft sand, and the stunning Aegean views.

For those willing to venture further afield, Livadia Beach is a great option. Situated near Parikia, this long, sandy beach offers beautiful views of the island's landscape. It's a perfect spot for a quiet afternoon by the sea, especially in the mornings when the beach is nearly deserted. The calm, turquoise waters invite visitors to swim, and the surrounding landscape adds to the tranquil vibe of the beach.

Lastly, Kalogeros Beach, located on the eastern side of Paros, is a hidden gem for those who love nature. The beach is known for its therapeutic mud, which has been used for centuries as a natural remedy for skin ailments. The beach is surrounded by rocky hills, and the waters are crystal-clear, making it perfect for a relaxing swim after covering yourself in the mineral-rich mud. It's a quieter, less commercialized spot, making it ideal for those looking to escape the busy tourist areas.

Paros' hidden beaches provide an excellent opportunity for visitors to experience the island's natural beauty in a more intimate and serene setting. Whether you're looking for seclusion, natural beauty, or the perfect place to swim and relax, Paros has a beach to fit your needs.

Cycling Through Ancient Villages and Olive Groves

One of the best ways to experience the true essence of Paros is by cycling through its picturesque villages and ancient landscapes. The island's diverse terrain, with its mix of coastal roads, quiet mountain paths, and traditional villages, provides the perfect setting for a cycling adventure that offers both exercise and scenic beauty. As you pedal through Paros, you'll discover some of the most charming corners of the island, from ancient ruins to lush olive groves, all while taking in the natural beauty that defines Paros.

The island's relatively flat terrain makes it an ideal destination for cycling, whether you're a beginner or an experienced cyclist. There are several bike rental shops in Parikia and Naoussa, offering a variety of bikes including road bikes, mountain bikes, and e-bikes for those looking to explore with a little extra help. Many of the routes are well-marked and easy to follow, making cycling an accessible way to explore Paros at your own pace.

One of the most popular cycling routes is the ride from Parikia to Aliki, a charming village located on the southern tip of the island. The ride is around 13 km and takes you through olive groves, rolling hills, and quaint, traditional villages where time seems to stand still. As you cycle through the peaceful landscape, you'll pass by small chapels and traditional farmhouses, giving you a true sense of local life. Along the way, there are plenty of opportunities to stop and admire the views of the Aegean Sea or take a break at one of the village cafes, where you can enjoy a refreshing glass of iced tea or a traditional Greek coffee.

The village of Lefkes, Located in the hills, is a must-see for cyclists looking for a more challenging route. About 10 km from Naoussa, Lefkes is known for its narrow, winding streets, traditional whitewashed houses, and stunning panoramic views of the island. The route up to Lefkes is a bit more challenging, with a steady incline that rewards cyclists with incredible views once they reach the village. Once in Lefkes, you can explore its cobblestone streets, visit the Church of Agia Triada, or relax in the village square with a cool drink.

For those interested in cycling through Paros' agricultural landscape, there's no better way to experience it than by pedaling through the island's famous olive groves. Paros has been producing olives for centuries, and the groves are still an important part of island life today. As you cycle through these verdant expanses, you'll pass by ancient olive trees, many of which are hundreds of years old, and you may even have the chance to stop and learn about the traditional methods of olive oil production. Some of the local farms offer tours, where you can taste the high-quality olive oil and learn about the island's agricultural heritage.

Cycling tours are also available for those who prefer a guided experience. These tours often include stops at some of Paros' most significant historical and cultural sites, such as the Ancient Marble Quarries near Marmara, where Paros' famous marble was once mined. Some tours also include visits to local wineries, where you can enjoy a glass of local wine after a day of cycling through the island's vineyards and olive groves.

Whether you're cycling solo or on a guided tour, Paros offers an unforgettable cycling experience, allowing you to explore its natural beauty, traditional villages, and rich cultural history from a completely unique perspective.

Local Food Secrets: Where to Find the Best Souvlaki

One of the joys of visiting Paros is experiencing its delicious local cuisine, and if there's one thing you should not miss, it's the island's take on souvlaki—a beloved Greek dish that has been adapted in unique ways across the islands. Souvlaki is a simple yet satisfying meal, consisting of grilled skewers of meat (typically pork, chicken, or lamb), served with pita bread, fresh vegetables, and a side of tangy tzatziki sauce. While you'll find souvlaki all over Greece, Paros offers some truly special versions of this iconic dish that are a must-try for food lovers.

Where to Find the Best Souvlaki on Paros

Souvlaki Loukoum (Parikia)

For an authentic, locally loved souvlaki experience, head to Souvlaki Loukoum in Parikia. This small, family-run joint is a favorite among locals and tourists alike, known for its perfectly grilled meat and fresh ingredients. The souvlaki is served in a warm, soft pita with crispy fries, fresh tomatoes, onions, and a dollop of homemade tzatziki. The real secret here is the marinade, which imparts a unique flavor to the grilled meat, making each bite a delight.

- **Price Range**: €4–€8 for a souvlaki wrap.
- **Distance**: Located in the heart of Parikia, just a short walk from the port.
- **Specialty**: Pork souvlaki with crispy fries, homemade tzatziki, and fresh pita.

To Souvlaki tou Psara (Naoussa)

For a slightly elevated souvlaki experience, visit To Souvlaki tou Psara in the town of Naoussa. This spot offers a range of grilled meats, but it's their souvlaki that keeps customers coming back for more. The skewers are tender, flavorful, and served with a side of fresh vegetables and pita bread. The unique addition of grilled halloumi cheese adds a savory twist, and their homemade sauces bring everything together beautifully.

- **Price Range**: €6–€12 for a souvlaki plate.
- **Distance**: Located in Naoussa's central square, within walking distance of the harbor.

- **Specialty**: Souvlaki with grilled halloumi and homemade sauces.

Pita Gyros & Souvlaki (Aliki)

If you're exploring the southern part of the island, Pita Gyros & Souvlaki in Aliki is a fantastic place to stop for a quick and delicious souvlaki meal. Known for its friendly service and fresh ingredients, this small eatery serves up classic Greek souvlaki in a laid-back, no-frills environment. The pita is always fresh, and the meat is tender and perfectly cooked. Be sure to try the Greek-style tzatziki—it's the perfect complement to the warm, flavorful souvlaki.

- **Price Range**: €4–€6 for a souvlaki wrap.
- **Distance**: 15 minutes by car from Parikia, located in the village of Aliki.
- **Specialty**: Simple, classic souvlaki with tangy tzatziki and fresh pita.

Taverna Glafkos (Piso Livadi)

For a more traditional experience, head to Taverna Glafkos in Piso Livadi. This family-run taverna is known for its authentic Greek cuisine, and while it offers a full menu of delicious dishes, their souvlaki is a standout. The skewers are grilled to perfection and served with a side of warm pita, homemade dips, and a salad of fresh vegetables. Dining here also gives you the opportunity to enjoy the peaceful atmosphere of Piso Livadi, with its views of the sea and nearby fishing boats.

- **Price Range**: €10–€15 for a souvlaki plate with sides.

- **Distance**: About 15 km from Parikia, located in Piso Livadi.
- **Specialty**: Traditional souvlaki served with a Greek salad and a side of local wines.

Zorba's (Naoussa)

Another excellent souvlaki option in Naoussa is Zorba's, a lively spot where you can enjoy classic Greek fast food in a fun, welcoming environment. The souvlaki here is freshly made with tender grilled meat, served in a warm pita with a variety of toppings like tomatoes, onions, lettuce, and tzatziki. Zorba's also offers a selection of Greek salads and side dishes, which pair perfectly with the savory souvlaki.

- **Price Range**: €5–€9 for a souvlaki wrap or plate.
- **Distance**: Located near Naoussa's main square.
- **Specialty**: Classic souvlaki with a side of Greek salad and fresh pita.

What Makes Paros' Souvlaki Special?

The secret to the exceptional souvlaki on Paros lies in the island's locally sourced ingredients. The meat, whether it's pork, chicken, or lamb, is often sourced from local farms, giving it a distinct, fresh flavor that sets it apart from souvlaki served elsewhere. Additionally, Paros' homemade pita bread, freshly baked on the island, is the perfect complement to the grilled meats, adding a soft and slightly crispy texture that enhances the overall experience.

Tzatziki, the classic Greek yogurt-based dip, is another key ingredient that elevates the souvlaki here. Each establishment takes pride in its own version of tzatziki, with a blend of garlic, cucumber, and herbs that adds a refreshing kick to the dish. The Greek fries, often served alongside the souvlaki or wrapped inside the pita, are crispy on the outside, fluffy on the inside, and make for a perfect addition to the meal.

For those with a taste for adventure, many souvlaki shops on Paros offer unique twists on the traditional souvlaki, such as adding grilled halloumi cheese, eggplant, or even spicy feta to the mix, giving a fresh take on the classic dish while maintaining its beloved flavors.

Chapter 4
Naxos – The Heart of the Cyclades

Image by Stefanos Nt on Unsplash

Ancient Temples and the Portara: A Historical Journey

Naxos, the largest island in the Cyclades, is rich in history and culture, offering a glimpse into the ancient world. The island is home to some of the most important archaeological sites in Greece, including the Portara—one of the most iconic monuments in the Cyclades. Visiting these historical sites is like stepping back in time, offering a deeper connection to Greece's ancient past.

The Portara, a massive marble doorway that stands alone on the islet of Palatia, is the most recognizable landmark of Naxos. This impressive structure dates back to the 6th century BCE and was originally part of a temple dedicated to the god Apollo. The temple, which was never completed, was meant to be one of the largest and most magnificent in the ancient world. Today, only the monumental entrance remains, but it stands as a testament to the grandeur and ambition of the ancient Greeks.

Standing at the Portara, you're treated to stunning panoramic views of the Naxos Town (Chora) and the surrounding Aegean Sea. The sight is especially magical at sunset, when the golden light bathes the marble structure and the sky is painted in hues of orange and pink. The Portara is an unforgettable experience and offers the perfect opportunity to reflect on the island's long and storied history. While at the site, take a moment to appreciate the historical significance of this grand structure, which still stands tall after centuries of change.

The history of Naxos doesn't end with the Portara. The island is dotted with ancient temples, ruins, and statues, many of which are still being uncovered by archaeologists. The Temple of Demeter at

Sangri is another fascinating site that offers insight into Naxos' religious practices in antiquity. This temple, built in the 6th century BCE, was dedicated to Demeter, the goddess of agriculture, and is notable for its well-preserved foundation and beautiful marble architecture. Visitors can walk through the ruins and imagine what life was like for the ancient inhabitants of Naxos, who revered their gods with grand temples and rituals.

For history buffs and anyone looking to connect with the ancient past, Naxos offers an immersive experience that combines stunning archaeological sites with breathtaking landscapes. Whether you're exploring the Portara or hiking to the Temple of Demeter, you'll feel a sense of awe as you stand on the same ground that has witnessed thousands of years of history unfold.

Naxian Cuisine: From Kitron to Fresh Seafood

Naxos is not only a paradise for history lovers and nature enthusiasts but also a culinary haven. The island's rich agricultural heritage, combined with its proximity to the Aegean Sea, results in a vibrant food scene that features both traditional Greek dishes and local specialties. Whether you're savoring the island's fresh seafood or sipping on its famous liqueur, **Kitron**, Naxos offers a feast for the senses.

Naxos' Fresh Seafood

Being an island, Naxos is known for its exceptional seafood, and the surrounding waters are abundant with fresh fish and shellfish. If you're a seafood lover, you won't want to miss the opportunity to indulge in freshly caught octopus, squid, lobster, and sea bream.

One of the most beloved dishes is grilled octopus, often charred to perfection and served with a drizzle of olive oil, lemon, and herbs. The squid is also a favorite, either grilled or stuffed with rice and herbs, offering a delicious, savory bite. In the coastal villages, you'll find many seaside tavernas where you can sit with your feet in the sand while enjoying fresh seafood dishes, accompanied by a chilled glass of local white wine or ouzo.

Lobster spaghetti is another must-try in Naxos, where the sweet, tender lobster is paired with a rich tomato sauce and al dente pasta. It's a luxurious dish that showcases the island's bountiful seafood. Whether served in a traditional taverna or a high-end restaurant, this dish is an essential part of the Naxian dining experience.

Kitron: Naxos' Famous Liqueur

No trip to Naxos is complete without trying Kitron, the island's signature liqueur made from the leaves and fruit of the citron tree. This unique drink is distilled on the island and comes in three varieties: green, yellow, and clear—each offering a different level of sweetness and intensity.

The green variety is the sweetest and most popular, while the yellow has a more refined, citrusy flavor. The clear Kitron is the strongest of the three and has a more herbal taste. Many tavernas and restaurants on the island serve Kitron as an after-dinner digestif, often chilled or served over ice. It's the perfect way to end a meal and cool off after a long day of exploring. If you're interested in learning more about this unique spirit, you can visit the Kitron distillery in Margarita, where you can tour the facilities and taste the different varieties.

Local Cheese and Meat Specialties

Naxos is also known for its local cheeses, which are produced using traditional methods passed down through generations. One of the most famous cheeses on the island is Graviera, a hard, salty cheese made from sheep's milk that's often served as an appetizer or grated over pasta dishes. You'll also find Kasseri, a softer cheese with a mild, buttery flavor, often served with honey and nuts as part of a mezze platter.

In addition to cheese, Naxos offers a variety of meat dishes, including lamb, goat, and pork. One local specialty to try is lamb with artichokes, where tender lamb is slow-cooked with fresh artichokes, olive oil, garlic, and herbs—a dish that perfectly embodies the flavors of the island. Another must-try is Souvlaki Naxos-style, where the meat is marinated in herbs and grilled to perfection, often served with pita, tomatoes, and a dollop of tzatziki.

Fresh Fruits and Vegetables

Thanks to its fertile soil, Naxos produces an abundance of fresh fruits and vegetables, many of which find their way into local dishes. The island is especially known for its Naxian potatoes, which are prized for their creamy texture and rich flavor. These potatoes are often roasted or fried and served as a side dish with meat or fish.

The island's markets are filled with fresh olives, tomatoes, herbs, and lettuce, all grown on the island's fields. In summer, the markets burst with color as fresh peaches, figs, and watermelon are sold in abundance. A local salad of tomatoes, cucumbers, olives, and feta cheese is a refreshing dish, perfect for a light lunch during the warm summer months.

Where to Experience Naxian Cuisine

The best way to enjoy Naxian cuisine is to dine at one of the island's traditional tavernas, where locals gather for hearty meals and a relaxed atmosphere. In Chora, the capital of Naxos, there are plenty of tavernas serving up authentic Naxian dishes, as well as family-run restaurants offering a personal touch and intimate dining experience.

- **To Elliniko (Chora):** This traditional taverna is a favorite among locals and visitors alike, offering a wide variety of Naxian specialties, including lamb with artichokes, grilled seafood, and delicious vegetarian dishes made from fresh, local produce. The rustic setting, combined with the hearty meals, makes it an ideal spot for an authentic taste of Naxos.

- **Nissaki Restaurant (Naxos Town):** For a more upscale dining experience, Nissaki offers stunning views of the sea and a menu that combines the best of Naxian cuisine with contemporary flair. The restaurant specializes in seafood, with fresh catch-of-the-day dishes like grilled octopus and lobster, as well as classic Greek favorites with a modern twist.

- **Souvlaki Loukoum (Chora):** For a quick, casual meal, head to Souvlaki Loukoum for some of the island's best souvlaki. This small, local spot offers grilled meats in a pita with fresh toppings and creamy tzatziki sauce—perfect for those looking for a tasty and satisfying snack.

Naxian cuisine is all about simplicity, quality ingredients, and tradition, making every meal an enjoyable and memorable experience. Whether you're savoring fresh seafood by the sea or enjoying a slow-cooked lamb dish in a quiet taverna, you'll find that the island's food is as much a part of its charm as its stunning landscapes.

Hiking the Mountains and Exploring Hidden Valleys

Naxos, with its rugged mountains, lush valleys, and diverse landscapes, is a hiker's paradise—offering some of the most scenic and rewarding trails in the Cyclades. While the island is often known for its beautiful beaches and historic sites, the true heart of Naxos lies in its interior. Here, you'll find hidden valleys, ancient villages, and pristine nature that will make you feel like you're stepping into a different world. Whether you're an avid hiker or simply looking for a relaxing stroll through nature, Naxos offers a range of hikes for every level of experience.

Hiking to Mount Zas: The Highest Peak in the Cyclades

The crown jewel of Naxos' hiking trails is the ascent to Mount Zas, the highest peak in the Cyclades, standing at an impressive 1,004 meters (3,294 feet). The hike to the top is a rewarding challenge, offering spectacular panoramic views of Naxos and the surrounding islands. Mount Zas is not only a great hiking destination, but it also holds mythological significance—it is said to be the home of the ancient Greek god Zeus, where he was raised as a child.

The hiking route to Mount Zas begins in the village of Filoti, located at the base of the mountain. From here, the trail winds through dense pine forests, rocky terrain, and winding paths that take you higher and higher up the slopes. The hike is moderate in difficulty, but the incredible views and unique landscapes make the effort worthwhile. As you climb, you'll pass through ancient olive groves, the smell of wild herbs in the air, and picturesque villages tucked away in the valleys.

Upon reaching the summit, you're treated to an awe-inspiring 360-degree view of Naxos, with its dramatic coastlines, lush valleys, and distant islands stretching out in all directions. The hike to Mount Zas is one of the best ways to experience the island's natural beauty, and the sense of accomplishment you'll feel when you reach the top is unparalleled.

- **Difficulty**: Moderate to challenging
- **Distance**: 8 km (5 miles) round trip
- **Duration**: 3–4 hours round trip
- **Specialty**: Stunning panoramic views, mythological significance, challenging but rewarding.

The Valley of Tragea: A Peaceful Escape

For those looking for a more tranquil and scenic hike, the Valley of Tragea is a hidden gem. This lush, fertile valley is located in the central part of the island and is surrounded by olive groves, citrus orchards, and ancient stone walls. The hike through the valley takes you through small, peaceful villages such as Kinidaros and Damarionas, where time seems to stand still. These traditional villages are perfect for those wanting to experience the quiet side of Naxos, away from the tourist crowds.

As you walk through Tragea, you'll encounter several ancient churches and chapels, each with its own history and charm. The valley is also home to many old windmills, which once powered grain production on the island. The natural beauty of the area is enhanced by the constant sound of birdsong and the scent of wildflowers and herbs that line the path. For a more cultural experience, consider visiting one of the local tavernas to taste Naxian specialties, or stop in at a local olive oil farm to learn about the island's ancient olive oil production.

- **Difficulty**: Easy to moderate
- **Distance**: 5–10 km (3–6 miles), depending on the route
- **Duration**: 2–3 hours
- **Specialty**: Peaceful atmosphere, traditional villages, ancient churches and windmills.

The Old Path to Chalki: A Journey Through History

Another fantastic hike is the ancient path that leads from Filoti to Chalki, one of the most beautiful and traditional villages on Naxos. This ancient route, which was once used by the locals to travel between villages, is a relatively easy and scenic walk. The path takes you through rolling hills, olive groves, and ancient terraced fields, offering stunning views of the island's natural beauty.

The route is not just scenic but also culturally rich. As you make your way towards Chalki, you'll pass by ancient temples and cultural landmarks, including the Temple of Demeter, one of the most important archaeological sites on the island. Once you reach

Chalki, you'll be greeted by the charming narrow streets and traditional Cycladic architecture of the village. Chalki is also home to the famous Kitron distillery, where you can learn about and taste the island's unique liqueur, Kitron.

- **Difficulty**: Easy to moderate
- **Distance**: 4 km (2.5 miles) one-way
- **Duration**: 1–2 hours
- **Specialty**: Ancient paths, cultural sites, scenic beauty, Kitron tasting.

Exploring the Hidden Valleys of Naxos

In addition to the popular hiking routes, Naxos is filled with hidden valleys and secluded paths that offer a quieter, more introspective way to experience the island. These valleys, often surrounded by ancient olive trees and vineyards, are perfect for those looking to escape the crowds and immerse themselves in nature. Many of the trails are located in the southern and eastern parts of the island, where you'll encounter fewer tourists and more untouched, natural beauty.

The hidden valleys offer an incredible opportunity to experience Naxos' true rural life. As you walk through these peaceful areas, you'll encounter ancient stone villages, winding paths, and traditional farmhouses. Some of these areas are also home to wildlife, such as goats, rabbits, and birds, and the natural landscape offers some of the island's best opportunities for wildlife photography.

- **Difficulty**: Easy to moderate

- **Distance**: Varies depending on the route
- **Duration**: Varies
- **Specialty**: Seclusion, natural beauty, rural villages, wildlife encounters.

Relaxation in the Quiet Villages: A Local's Perspective

While Naxos has much to offer in terms of historical sites, adventurous hiking, and stunning beaches, the true magic of the island lies in its quiet villages, where time moves slower and life is still deeply connected to the rhythms of nature. These traditional villages offer a rare opportunity to experience the authentic charm of Naxos, away from the crowds and hustle of more tourist-heavy areas. Whether you're looking to unwind, explore, or simply enjoy the island's laid-back lifestyle, these villages provide the perfect escape.

Margarita: A Village Steeped in Tradition

Located in the central hills of Naxos, Margarita is a charming village that offers a peaceful retreat from the more bustling parts of the island. The village is known for its traditional stone houses, narrow streets, and warm, welcoming locals. Here, you can experience a slower pace of life, where the community still works the land, farming olive groves and vineyards that have been passed down through generations.

Strolling through Margarita, you'll encounter small, family-run tavernas, where locals serve hearty meals made from fresh, locally grown ingredients. One of the highlights of the village is its traditional olive oil farms, which have been producing some of the finest olive oil in the Cyclades for centuries. Visiting one of these farms is a great way to connect with the island's agricultural heritage and learn about the ancient methods of olive oil production.

In the evenings, the village square comes alive with locals enjoying a drink at the local café or chatting with friends. The air is filled with the scent of blooming jasmine and the sound of distant church bells. Margarita offers a true sense of Naxian hospitality, where visitors can slow down and immerse themselves in the island's authentic lifestyle.

- **Specialty**: Olive oil production, traditional tavernas, peaceful village atmosphere.

- **Distance**: About 9 km from Chora (20 minutes by car).

- **Perfect for**: Relaxing strolls, enjoying local food, and experiencing rural island life.

Filoti: A Mountain Village with a View

At the foot of Mount Zas, Filoti is one of the largest and most picturesque villages on Naxos. Known for its charming stone houses, winding alleyways, and stunning views, Filoti offers a unique combination of natural beauty and traditional Cycladic architecture. The village is a great place to explore on foot, as its cobblestone streets lead you to hidden squares and quaint cafes where you can rest and enjoy the local flavor.

Filoti's main square is the heart of the village, where locals gather in the evenings to chat, drink coffee, and enjoy each other's company. The square is surrounded by traditional tavernas serving local specialties such as Naxian cheese and lamb. One of the best things about Filoti is its proximity to Mount Zas, which makes it a perfect base for hikers looking to climb the island's highest peak. After a day of hiking, the village offers a tranquil place to relax and enjoy a well-earned meal.

Filoti is also home to several ancient churches, including the Church of Agios Georgios, where you can experience the quiet spirituality of the village. Whether you're looking to hike, explore, or simply unwind, Filoti offers a welcoming and serene environment where you can disconnect from the outside world.

- **Specialty**: Stone architecture, hiking to Mount Zas, peaceful village square.

- **Distance**: About 16 km from Chora (25 minutes by car).

- **Perfect for**: Hikers, history lovers, and those seeking a peaceful retreat.

Chalki: A Village Frozen in Time

One of the most picturesque villages on the island is Chalki, located in the central part of Naxos. The village is surrounded by lush vineyards and olive groves, creating a serene and tranquil atmosphere. Chalki has managed to preserve its traditional charm, with its narrow streets, whitewashed houses, and quaint shops. The village is famous for its Kitron distillery, where the island's signature liqueur is produced using the leaves of the citron tree.

Chalki's main square is lined with cafes and tavernas, offering a perfect spot to relax and watch the world go by. The village is also home to the impressive Church of Panagia and a few small museums dedicated to the island's history and culture. As you stroll through Chalki, you'll notice the peaceful ambiance, with locals tending to their daily activities and chatting with visitors.

The village's relatively quiet pace makes it an ideal place for a laid-back afternoon, whether you're enjoying a traditional Greek coffee or sampling local cheese at a family-run shop. The surrounding countryside is perfect for short walks, where you can discover the island's wildflowers, olive trees, and old stone walls that have withstood centuries of change.

- **Specialty**: Kitron liqueur, traditional architecture, tranquil village life.
- **Distance**: About 16 km from Chora (25 minutes by car).
- **Perfect for**: Relaxing, local food exploration, and enjoying the calm atmosphere.

Vallindras: A Secluded Escape

For those who seek ultimate tranquility, Vallindras is one of the most peaceful and secluded villages on Naxos. Located in the northern part of the island, Vallindras is less frequented by tourists, making it the perfect place to disconnect and immerse yourself in the natural beauty of Naxos. The village is small but charming, with only a handful of houses, an ancient olive press, and a few local cafes.

The surrounding area is filled with hiking paths that take you through mountainous terrain and pine forests, offering some of the best views on the island. The village is particularly beautiful at sunrise, when the soft morning light bathes the landscape in a golden glow, and the only sounds you'll hear are the rustling of leaves and the calls of birds.

If you're looking for complete solitude, Vallindras offers an authentic Naxian experience—where you can spend the day exploring the countryside, visiting traditional olive farms, and enjoying the simplicity of rural life.

- **Specialty**: Quiet, secluded environment, nature walks, traditional olive farming.
- **Distance**: About 13 km from Chora (20 minutes by car).
- **Perfect for**: Solitude, nature lovers, and those seeking a peaceful retreat.

Chapter 5
Milos – The Island of Color

The Stunning Beaches of Sarakiniko and Firiplaka

Image by David Tip on Unsplash

Milos, known as "The Island of Color", is home to some of the most stunning and unique beaches in Greece. The island's volcanic history has created a dramatic landscape with striking white cliffs, crystal-clear waters, and soft sandy shores. Among the island's many beaches, Sarakiniko and Firiplaka stand out as two of the most iconic and visually stunning spots.

Sarakiniko Beach: Moon-like Landscapes and Crystal-Clear Waters

One of the most photographed beaches in all of Greece, **Sarakiniko** is famous for its otherworldly landscape, resembling the surface of the moon. The beach is set against a backdrop of bright white **rock formations** that have been eroded over time, creating a surreal and striking scene. The rocks are smooth and almost alien in appearance, making this beach feel like a place outside of time and reality.

The water at Sarakiniko is a brilliant shade of turquoise, and the beach itself is relatively shallow, making it perfect for swimming, snorkeling, and sunbathing. While the beach is rocky, the stunning views and unique atmosphere make it worth the effort. Visitors often climb the rock formations to get the best views of the surrounding coastline, or they can walk along the smooth, white stone surfaces that lead down to the water.

Sarakiniko is also a great spot for **photography**, with the contrast of the white rock, blue waters, and bright skies providing a dramatic backdrop. Whether you're looking to relax and take in the view or explore the fascinating rock formations, Sarakiniko offers a magical experience unlike any other beach in Greece.

- **Price Range**: Free entry (parking may have a small fee in high season).
- **Specialty**: Moon-like landscapes, turquoise waters, ideal for photography.
- **Perfect for**: Exploring rock formations, swimming, and stunning photo ops.

Firiplaka Beach: Soft Sand and Dramatic Cliffs

Another beautiful beach on Milos is Firiplaka, located on the southern coast of the island. Firiplaka is a long, sandy beach with crystal-clear waters, making it ideal for a day of relaxation and swimming. What makes this beach unique is the dramatic cliffs that surround it, which have been shaped by the island's volcanic activity. The cliffs are layered in various shades of red, yellow, and orange, creating a colorful and striking backdrop to the soft golden sand.

The water at Firiplaka is warm and shallow, making it perfect for families and those looking to unwind in a peaceful setting. The beach is also less crowded than Sarakiniko, providing a more tranquil experience. Firiplaka is known for its natural beauty, and visitors often spend hours lounging by the water, enjoying the stunning views, and taking in the vibrant colors of the cliffs.

For those who enjoy a more active day at the beach, Firiplaka offers excellent opportunities for snorkeling, with clear waters that are home to a variety of marine life. The beach is also a popular spot for windsurfing and kiteboarding, thanks to the steady winds in the area. You'll also find a couple of beachside tavernas where you can enjoy fresh seafood and traditional Greek dishes with a view of the sea.

- **Price Range**: Free entry (sunbeds and umbrellas may be rented for €10–€20).
- **Specialty**: Sandy beach, dramatic cliffs, ideal for swimming and snorkeling.
- **Perfect for**: Relaxing, water sports, and beachside dining.

The Ancient Catacombs and Roman Theater

Milos is not only known for its breathtaking beaches and natural beauty but also for its rich history. The island is home to several ancient archaeological sites, and two of the most fascinating are the Ancient Catacombs and the Roman Theater. These sites offer a glimpse into the island's historical significance, dating back to the early Christian and Roman periods.

The Ancient Catacombs of Milos

The Ancient Catacombs of Milos are one of the most important and well-preserved early Christian sites in Greece. Located near the village of Tripiti, these catacombs date back to the 1st century AD and were used as burial sites by early Christians during a time of persecution. The catacombs consist of a series of interconnected underground chambers carved into the soft volcanic rock, with narrow passageways that wind through the complex.

The catacombs were used by the early Christian community as both a place of worship and a burial ground, with many tombs still visible along the walls. The walls are adorned with early Christian symbols, such as crosses, fish, and good shepherds, which provide insight into the religious practices of the time. The site is also notable for its well-preserved frescoes, some of which have been restored and are displayed in the nearby Milos Archaeological Museum.

Visitors can take a guided tour of the catacombs to learn about their fascinating history and the role they played in the early Christian period. The atmosphere inside is cool and quiet, offering a peaceful space for reflection on the island's rich cultural heritage.

- **Price Range**: Entrance fee is usually €4–€6.
- **Specialty**: Early Christian history, well-preserved catacombs, fascinating frescoes.
- **Perfect for**: History enthusiasts, those interested in early Christian archaeology.

The Roman Theater of Milos

Located in the village of Tripiti, not far from the catacombs, the Roman Theater of Milos is another remarkable historical site on the island. The theater, which dates back to the 1st century BC, was once an important venue for performances during the Roman period. While it may not be as large or as famous as other Roman theaters in Greece, it is still an impressive site and a testament to the island's importance during antiquity.

The Roman Theater of Milos was carved into the hillside, with seats made from local stone arranged in a semi-circular pattern. The theater once held up to 7,000 spectators, and although much of it has been eroded by time, the remains still offer a clear view of the theater's layout. The most striking feature of the theater is its stage area, which still retains some of the original steps and columns.

While the theater is not in its original pristine condition, visitors can still imagine the grandeur of the performances that took place here. The location offers spectacular views of the surrounding countryside and coastline, making it a perfect spot to visit for both its historical significance and its scenic beauty.

- **Price Range**: Free entry (small fee for the catacombs nearby).
- **Specialty**: Roman history, scenic views, intimate atmosphere.
- **Perfect for**: History lovers, those interested in Roman architecture and ancient theaters.

Both the **Ancient Catacombs** and the **Roman Theater** provide fascinating insights into the island's past and its role in early Christian and Roman history. Visiting these sites is a great way to connect with Milos' rich cultural heritage, while also enjoying the peaceful and scenic surroundings.

Secluded Caves and Cliffside Villages: Uncovering Milos' Secrets

Milos is a place of secrets, both natural and historical, where rugged cliffs, hidden caves, and picturesque villages offer a quiet retreat from the more crowded parts of the island. While the beaches of Milos often take center stage, there are many other hidden treasures to discover, including secluded caves, dramatic cliffs, and quiet villages perched on the island's hillsides. Exploring these remote spots provides a deeper connection to Milos' authentic charm, away from the bustling crowds.

Kleftiko: A Hidden Gem Accessible Only by Boat

One of the most famous and isolated spots on Milos is Kleftiko, a dramatic cave system and beach only accessible by boat. This isolated location, once a pirate hideout, is known for its towering white rock formations, crystal-clear waters, and hidden sea caves. The name Kleftiko comes from the word "kleftis," meaning "thief," as pirates used to use the caves as a safe haven to stash their loot and avoid detection.

The area is renowned for its unique geological formations, including stark white cliffs that rise dramatically from the turquoise sea, creating a surreal landscape. Visitors can explore the caves by boat or kayak, and some tours even offer opportunities to swim in the sea caves. The waters around Kleftiko are calm and shallow, perfect for snorkeling and exploring the vibrant marine life, including colorful fish, sea urchins, and the occasional octopus.

Kleftiko is a must-see for those looking to experience the natural beauty of Milos at its most untouched. While it's a bit challenging to reach (most visitors take boat tours from Adamas or Pollonia), the stunning scenery and peaceful surroundings make it well worth the trip.

- **Price Range**: Boat tours from €20–€40 per person.
- **Specialty**: Secluded caves, dramatic cliffs, crystal-clear waters.
- **Perfect for**: Nature lovers, photographers, adventurers.

The Caves of Milos: Exploring the Island's Hidden Secrets

Beyond Kleftiko, Milos is home to several **hidden sea caves** and grottoes that are waiting to be discovered. These caves, carved into the island's volcanic cliffs, are often inaccessible by land and can only be reached by boat, making them a truly secluded experience.

One of the most famous cave systems on the island is the **Sykia Cave**, located on the southern coast of Milos. This massive cave features a **large collapsed roof**, creating a natural skylight that allows sunlight to pour into the cave below, illuminating the turquoise waters. The cave is an awe-inspiring sight, and many boat tours around the island will stop here to allow guests to swim in the cave's cool waters. The atmosphere inside the cave is serene, with the sound of lapping waves and the faint smell of saltwater filling the air.

In addition to Sykia, there are several smaller caves scattered around Milos' coast that offer an intimate experience with nature. These secluded spots are perfect for those looking for a quiet escape, where you can enjoy the beauty of the island in peace, away from the crowds. Exploring these caves by boat or kayak offers a unique perspective of Milos' rugged coastline, and the opportunity to swim in some of the most pristine waters in Greece.

- **Price Range**: Boat rental or tours typically cost €30–€80 for a half-day tour.
- **Specialty**: Secluded sea caves, dramatic cliffs, peaceful ambiance.
- **Perfect for**: Adventure seekers, nature lovers, and photographers.

The Cliffside Villages: Tranquil Villages Above the Sea

Milos is also home to several **cliffside villages** that offer stunning views of the Aegean Sea and a peaceful retreat from the island's more tourist-heavy areas. These villages are perfect for those looking to experience authentic island life while enjoying breathtaking scenery.

- **Plaka**, the island's capital, is one of the most picturesque villages on Milos. Perched on a hilltop, Plaka offers sweeping views of the sea and the surrounding islands. The village is characterized by its narrow streets, whitewashed houses, and vibrant bougainvillea, creating a charming and peaceful atmosphere. Walking through Plaka, you'll encounter small shops selling local crafts, traditional tavernas offering delicious Naxian cuisine, and quiet cafes where you can relax and enjoy the views.

- **Triovasalos**, located just a few kilometers from Plaka, is another cliffside village known for its traditional architecture and tranquil ambiance. This village is less visited by tourists, making it a perfect place for those looking for a quiet escape. The village is Located among the hills, with narrow stone paths leading to secluded corners and small, family-run shops.

- **Pollonia**, located on the northeast coast of the island, is a small, peaceful fishing village that offers beautiful views of the sea and nearby islands. While it's more developed than some of the island's other villages, it still maintains a quiet, laid-back atmosphere. The village is home to several restaurants serving fresh seafood, as well as charming little shops where you can purchase local products and souvenirs.

The cliffside villages of Milos offer a unique way to experience the island, providing the perfect mix of **natural beauty, peaceful surroundings**, and **traditional Cycladic architecture**. Whether you're staying in one of the villages or simply passing through, these picturesque settlements offer the ideal setting for a relaxing and authentic Greek experience.

- **Specialty**: Traditional Cycladic architecture, stunning sea views, peaceful atmosphere.
- **Perfect for**: Photography, exploring local culture, and relaxing in peaceful surroundings.

Sailing Around the Island: Exploring by Boat

One of the best ways to truly experience the beauty and uniqueness of **Milos** is by boat. Sailing around the island allows you to access some of the most hidden and spectacular spots that are difficult to reach by land. From secluded beaches and sea caves to dramatic cliffs and stunning coastlines, a boat trip around Milos offers an unforgettable perspective of the island's diverse natural beauty. Whether you choose a leisurely sailing tour or opt for a private boat charter, exploring Milos by sea is an experience that should not be missed.

Discovering Hidden Beaches and Caves

The island's coast is dotted with hidden beaches and dramatic sea caves that can only be accessed by boat. While beaches like **Sarakiniko** and **Firiplaka** are well-known, many of the most beautiful and secluded spots can only be reached by sea. Some of these beaches are so isolated that they feel like your own private paradise.

One of the most famous spots to visit by boat is **Kleftiko**, a secluded bay with stunning white rock formations and crystal-clear waters. This spot, once used as a pirate hideout, is surrounded by towering cliffs and hidden caves, which you can explore by boat or kayak. The waters here are perfect for swimming and snorkeling, with vibrant marine life and clear visibility. Many boat tours stop at Kleftiko for a few hours, allowing you to swim, explore the caves, and enjoy the peace and beauty of this hidden gem.

Another incredible destination that's best explored by boat is **Sykia Cave**, a massive sea cave with a collapsed roof that lets the sunlight pour in, creating an ethereal atmosphere. You can swim into the cave, marvel at the natural light filtering through the hole in the ceiling, and enjoy the tranquility of the secluded waters. The entrance to the cave is narrow, but once inside, the vast expanse is truly awe-inspiring.

Private Boat Charters: Customizable and Exclusive

For those seeking a more personalized and luxurious experience, **private boat charters** are an excellent option. These charters allow you to design your own itinerary, visiting the places that interest you most at your own pace. Whether you want to spend the day exploring **remote beaches**, **hidden coves**, or enjoying a **sunset cruise** along the coastline, a private boat charter offers a unique way to see the island.

Private boat tours can be customized to suit your preferences. You can choose to spend the day **snorkeling**, **swimming**, or **fishing**, or simply enjoy a relaxing cruise around the island with a glass of wine in hand. Some charters even offer a crewed experience, where you'll have a captain and crew to take care of everything, allowing you to fully relax and enjoy the experience.

Many boat companies offer half-day or full-day charters, and the cost will vary depending on the type of boat, the duration of the tour, and the number of people. Prices generally start at around €300 for a half-day tour and can go up to €1,000 or more for a full-day, private luxury boat experience.

- **Price Range**: €300–€1,000 for private charters, depending on the boat and duration.
- **Specialty**: Customizable itineraries, private and luxury experiences, stunning coastal views.

Sailing Tours: A Great Way to Meet Fellow Travelers

For those looking for a more social experience, joining a **sailing tour** is a great way to explore Milos while meeting other travelers. These tours typically include stops at some of the island's most famous beaches and caves, as well as lesser-known spots that are only accessible by sea. The tours often include activities like **swimming**, **snorkeling**, and even **snack breaks** on the beach, allowing you to enjoy the full range of experiences that Milos has to offer.

Sailing tours usually last anywhere from 4 to 8 hours, and many of them provide refreshments or meals on board, adding to the relaxed, vacation-like atmosphere. Most tours are small group experiences, meaning you'll get to interact with fellow passengers while enjoying the sights, sounds, and tastes of Milos. Some tours even offer themed experiences, such as **sunset cruises** or **wine-tasting tours**, allowing you to explore the island in a more unique and immersive way.

Many companies offer day trips that include stops at **Kleftiko**, **Sykia Cave**, and other iconic locations around the island. Prices for group sailing tours typically range from €50–€80 per person, depending on the tour length and inclusions.

- **Price Range**: €50–€80 per person for group tours, based on duration and inclusions.
- **Specialty**: Small group experiences, snorkeling, and swimming stops at hidden beaches.
- **Perfect for**: Social travelers, those looking for an immersive sailing experience, and budget-conscious adventurers.

Sunset Cruises: The Perfect End to a Day in Milos

One of the most magical ways to experience Milos is by taking a **sunset cruise**. Watching the sun set over the **Aegean Sea** from the deck of a boat is an unforgettable experience. As the sun dips below the horizon, the island's cliffs and beaches are bathed in golden light, creating a truly breathtaking sight.

Sunset cruises typically depart in the late afternoon and last a few hours, giving you ample time to relax and take in the stunning views. Many sunset cruises also offer light appetizers and drinks, allowing you to enjoy a cocktail while watching the sky transform into vibrant shades of orange, pink, and purple. Some boats even offer the opportunity to swim in the warm waters of a secluded bay as the sun begins to set.

Whether you choose a private charter or a group tour, a **sunset cruise** is the perfect way to unwind and experience Milos from a completely different perspective. It's an ideal way to end a day of exploring the island, providing a peaceful and romantic atmosphere as you sail into the evening.

- **Price Range**: €50–€100 per person for group sunset cruises, or more for private tours.
- **Specialty**: Sunset views, relaxing atmosphere, swimming stops.
- **Perfect for**: Romantic couples, solo travelers, and anyone looking to unwind.

Chapter 6
Syros – The Cultural Hub

Ermoupoli: The Fusion of Neoclassical and Cycladic Architecture

Syros is the cultural heart of the Cyclades, a place where the past and present coexist harmoniously. Ermoupoli, the island's capital, is a stunning example of how Neoclassical and Cycladic architectural styles blend seamlessly together. The town offers an architectural journey that spans centuries, showcasing both Greek traditions and influences from the Venetians, French, and Ottomans who left their mark on the island.

When you walk through the streets of Ermoupoli, it feels as though you're stepping into a living museum. The town's Neoclassical buildings, with their grand facades, intricately designed balconies, and stately columns, give the town a sense of elegance and sophistication. Many of these buildings date back to the 19th century, when Syros flourished as a major commercial and cultural hub of the eastern Mediterranean.

One of the most impressive buildings in Ermoupoli is the Apollo Theater, a striking example of Neoclassical architecture. Built in the 19th century, the theater is modeled after the famous La Scala Opera House in Milan and is one of the oldest opera houses in Greece. The Apollo Theater is a symbol of Ermoupoli's cultural prominence during its heyday. The Miaouli Square, at the heart of the town, is another highlight, surrounded by grand Neoclassical buildings like the Town Hall and the Statue of Markos Vamvakaris—

a tribute to the famous Rembetiko singer who was born in Ermoupoli.

In contrast to the grandeur of Neoclassical architecture, the traditional Cycladic style is also very much present in Ermoupoli, especially in the older parts of the town. Whitewashed buildings, narrow alleyways, and colorful doorways create a warm, inviting atmosphere. These charming streets lead to hidden courtyards, cafes, and artisan shops that offer a more intimate glimpse of life in Syros. As you wander through the town, you'll notice how the Cycladic simplicity complements the more formal Neoclassical structures, creating a balance of elegance and warmth that is unique to Ermoupoli.

The juxtaposition of Neoclassical grandeur and Cycladic simplicity gives Ermoupoli a distinct personality, making it one of the most culturally rich towns in the Aegean. It's a place where history is preserved not only in museums and monuments but in the very architecture that fills the streets.

- **Specialty**: Neoclassical and Cycladic fusion, grand public buildings, elegant squares.
- **Perfect for**: Architecture lovers, history enthusiasts, and those who appreciate the beauty of Greek heritage.

Museums, Art Galleries, and Theatres

Syros is not only the cultural hub of the Cyclades because of its unique architecture but also for its thriving art scene, rich history, and preserved traditions. The island is home to several fascinating museums, art galleries, and theatres that showcase its rich cultural heritage, making it a must-visit for anyone looking to explore Greek history and art beyond the beaches.

The Archaeological Museum of Syros

One of the most important cultural institutions on the island is the Archaeological Museum of Syros, located in Ermoupoli. This museum offers an insightful journey into the island's ancient history, dating back to the Neolithic period. The museum's collection includes a wide array of artifacts found on the island, such as pottery, sculptures, and jewelry, which provide a glimpse into the daily life, religious practices, and trade routes of ancient Syros.

The most notable exhibit is the Cycladic figurines, small marble sculptures that are a hallmark of the Cycladic civilization. These minimalist, abstract figures are some of the most famous artifacts of ancient Greece and are known for their distinct form. The museum also houses an impressive collection of Roman and

Byzantine-era relics, as well as a number of medieval objects from Syros' time under Venetian and Ottoman rule.

A visit to the Archaeological Museum of Syros is essential for anyone interested in understanding the island's historical significance and the cultural influences that have shaped it over the millennia.

- **Price Range**: €3–€5 for entry.
- **Specialty**: Cycladic figurines, ancient pottery, Byzantine and Roman artifacts.
- **Perfect for**: History buffs, archaeology enthusiasts, and those interested in Greek ancient civilizations.

The Museum of Industrial History of Syros

A visit to the Museum of Industrial History of Syros offers a unique perspective on the island's role as a commercial hub in the 19th and early 20th centuries. Located in the Ermoupoli Industrial District, the museum tells the story of Syros' industrial past, particularly its thriving shipbuilding industry and the production of textiles and soap.

Syros played a significant role in the maritime and industrial history of Greece, with its shipyards providing ships for both the Greek navy and merchant fleets. The museum's collection includes old machinery, blueprints, and photographs that bring to life the island's industrial revolution and the evolution of labor and manufacturing during that time.

Visitors can explore the museum's exhibits to learn about the island's transformation from a quiet fishing village to a bustling industrial center. The museum's location in a former industrial complex provides an authentic experience, where you can see the original structures and machinery that powered Syros' growth during the 1800s.

- **Price Range**: €2–€4 for entry.
- **Specialty**: Shipbuilding history, industrial machinery, textile production.
- **Perfect for**: History enthusiasts, industrial history fans, and those interested in Greece's 19th-century growth.

The Syros Art Gallery

Syros is home to a burgeoning art scene, and the Syros Art Gallery (also known as the Gallery of Contemporary Art) is a must-visit for art lovers. Located in the heart of Ermoupoli, the gallery hosts a rotating collection of contemporary art from Greek and international artists. The gallery's exhibitions cover a wide range of media, from painting and sculpture to photography and installation art.

In addition to contemporary works, the Syros Art Gallery also showcases exhibitions dedicated to the island's artistic history, with a focus on the local culture and the influence of Syros on the arts throughout the centuries. The gallery frequently holds art openings, workshops, and cultural events, making it a dynamic space for creativity and community engagement.

Whether you're interested in exploring modern art or experiencing local artistic expressions, the Syros Art Gallery offers an engaging and thought-provoking experience for visitors.

- **Price Range**: Free entry, but donations are encouraged.

- **Specialty**: Contemporary Greek and international art, rotating exhibitions, workshops.

- **Perfect for**: Art lovers, culture seekers, and contemporary art enthusiasts.

The Apollo Theatre: A Cultural Landmark

No visit to Syros is complete without experiencing the grandeur of the Apollo Theatre in Ermoupoli. Opened in 1864, the Apollo Theatre is one of the oldest and most historically significant opera houses in Greece. The theatre's stunning Neoclassical design, with its intricate frescoes, golden balconies, and velvet seating, takes visitors back to the golden age of Greek culture. Modeled after the famous La Scala Opera House in Milan, the Apollo Theatre became a symbol of the island's cultural sophistication during the 19th century.

Today, the Apollo Theatre is a vibrant cultural hub, hosting opera performances, classical music concerts, ballet, and theatre productions. The building also serves as the venue for the Syros International Film Festival, which attracts artists and filmmakers from around the world. Attending a performance at the Apollo Theatre is a magical experience, and the theater's acoustic design ensures that every note resonates perfectly throughout the space.

- **Price Range**: Ticket prices vary depending on the performance.

- **Specialty**: Classical music, opera, theatre productions, cultural performances.

- **Perfect for**: Theatre-goers, music lovers, and those interested in Greek cultural landmarks.

Quiet Cafes and Artisan Shops: A Taste of Local Life

One of the most delightful aspects of visiting Syros is experiencing its local life through the many quiet cafes and artisan shops scattered throughout the island. While the island is known for its vibrant cultural heritage and historical landmarks, it is these small, intimate spots that truly offer a window into the heart of Syros. The atmosphere is relaxed, the pace is slower, and the people are incredibly friendly—making it the perfect place to unwind and enjoy the simple pleasures of island life.

Charming Cafes in Ermoupoli and Beyond

The town of Ermoupoli, with its Neoclassical architecture and vibrant streets, offers a variety of cozy cafes where you can spend hours sipping coffee, people-watching, and soaking in the ambiance. The cafes here are often hidden in quiet corners or tucked away in the narrow alleys, providing a peaceful escape from the more tourist-heavy areas.

- Kouchico Café (Ermoupoli): Located in the heart of Ermoupoli, Kouchico Café is a perfect blend of modernity and tradition. The stylish interior features local artwork and vintage furniture, creating a warm and inviting space. The café serves a variety of Greek coffee and international brews, along with freshly baked pastries and light bites. It's a great spot to relax and enjoy a slow-paced morning while reading a book or chatting with locals.

- Specialty: Greek coffee, homemade pastries, relaxed atmosphere.
- Perfect for: Coffee lovers, casual conversations, people-watching.

- Laoutari Café (Ermoupoli): Another must-visit café in Ermoupoli, Laoutari is known for its traditional Greek ambiance and its delicious coffee blends. The café serves a variety of homemade desserts, including baklava and kataifi, making it a great spot for indulging in classic Greek sweets. The café's outdoor seating area provides a beautiful view of the town, and the friendly staff make you feel right at home.
  - **Specialty**: Greek sweets, traditional coffee, outdoor seating with a view.
  - **Perfect for**: Desserts, people-watching, and enjoying the town's charm.

For those looking to explore quieter parts of Syros, the village of Ano Syros, perched on a hill above Ermoupoli, offers some quaint local cafes with breathtaking views. Enjoy your coffee while looking out over the Aegean Sea and the terracotta rooftops of the surrounding villages.

Artisan Shops: Handcrafted Treasures and Local Goods

Syros is known for its vibrant artisan community, and exploring the island's artisan shops is a wonderful way to experience the local culture and take home unique, handcrafted souvenirs. From jewelry and textiles to pottery and woodworking, the island's artisans create one-of-a-kind pieces that reflect the island's artistic heritage.

- Maria's Art and Jewelry Shop (Ermoupoli): For anyone interested in unique, locally made jewelry, Maria's Art and Jewelry Shop in Ermoupoli is a must-visit. The shop specializes in handmade jewelry crafted from silver, gold, and precious stones, often inspired by the island's natural surroundings. Whether you're looking for a special piece for yourself or a unique gift for someone else, Maria's creations are a beautiful reflection of the island's artistry.

    - Specialty: Handmade jewelry, precious stones, local craftsmanship.
    - Perfect for: Jewelry lovers, souvenir hunters, and those interested in local artisanship.

- Syros Handicrafts (Ermoupoli): If you're looking for traditional Greek textiles, Syros Handicrafts offers beautifully crafted items such as embroidered linens, woolen scarves, and handmade pottery. Many of these items are made using traditional techniques, and the shop is a great place to find high-quality, locally made goods that showcase the island's heritage.

    - **Specialty**: Handwoven textiles, embroidered linens, pottery.
    - **Perfect for**: Textile enthusiasts, home décor lovers, and those seeking unique souvenirs.

- The Art of Wood (Ano Syros): For a more rustic experience, head to The Art of Wood in the hilltop village of Ano Syros.

This charming workshop specializes in wooden crafts, including hand-carved figurines, furniture, and decorative pieces. Each item is carefully crafted by local artisans, and you can watch the craftsmen at work while learning about the techniques they use. It's a great place to find a unique and authentic keepsake that reflects the island's artistic roots.

- **Specialty**: Hand-carved wooden figurines, furniture, and décor.
- **Perfect for**: Collectors of handmade crafts, lovers of rustic design, and art enthusiasts.

The Art of Slow Living: Experiencing Syros' Quiet Side

Beyond the cafes and shops, the true beauty of Syros lies in the simple act of slowing down and embracing the island's slower pace of life. Take a leisurely walk through the narrow streets of Ermoupoli, stop for a drink in the town's square, or explore the hilltop village of Ano Syros, where time seems to have stopped. Here, you'll encounter local shopkeepers, friendly residents, and artisans who take pride in their craft and their island's heritage.

The island's laid-back atmosphere makes it the perfect place to escape the fast-paced world and embrace the art of slow living. Whether you're relaxing at a café with a cup of coffee, browsing through artisan shops for unique handmade goods, or simply enjoying a quiet walk through the town's historic neighborhoods, Syros offers a rich and fulfilling experience of Greek island life.

Exploring the Byzantine Pathways: Walking Through History

Syros is not just an island with beautiful beaches and charming villages; it's also a place where history is etched into its very landscape. One of the best ways to truly experience the island's cultural richness is by walking through its Byzantine pathways, which connect significant historical sites, ancient churches, and hidden corners of the island. These pathways not only offer a chance to explore the island's Byzantine heritage but also allow you to immerse yourself in the peaceful, timeless atmosphere that defines Syros.

The Byzantine Route of Ano Syros

Ano Syros, the island's medieval capital, is a perfect starting point for exploring the Byzantine pathways of Syros. This hilltop village, perched above Ermoupoli, offers a timeless atmosphere, with narrow, winding streets, whitewashed houses, and ancient buildings that have remained relatively unchanged for centuries. The village itself is a living museum of Syros' rich Byzantine and medieval history.

As you wander through the cobblestone streets of Ano Syros, you'll come across several historic churches, including the Church of St. George and the Cathedral of Saint Nicholas. The architecture of these churches is a testament to the Byzantine influence on the island. Their intricate stonework, frescoed ceilings, and wooden icons create an air of reverence and serenity, offering visitors a glimpse into the religious and cultural life of the past.

Walking through the narrow alleyways of Ano Syros, you'll encounter stone houses and hidden courtyards that have been preserved for centuries. The village's layout, with its steep hills and winding pathways, reflects the strategic positioning of this medieval settlement, which was built to offer protection from invaders.

One of the most fascinating aspects of Ano Syros is its Byzantine architecture, which is evident in the ancient fortified walls and watchtowers that still stand today. These structures, originally built to protect the village from pirate attacks and foreign invasions, offer an interesting contrast to the more modern architecture of Ermoupoli, showing the island's adaptability and resilience over the centuries.

- **Specialty**: Byzantine and medieval architecture, narrow cobbled streets, and ancient churches.
- **Perfect for**: History lovers, architecture enthusiasts, and those looking for a peaceful escape into the past.

The Byzantine Churches of Syros

Syros is home to several Byzantine churches that are scattered across the island, each one telling its own unique story. Some are located in the heart of the island's villages, while others are tucked away in more secluded spots. These churches are not just places of worship but also architectural masterpieces, with intricate mosaics, frescoes, and Byzantine-style iconography.

One of the most important Byzantine churches on the island is the Church of Agios Nikolaos in Ermoupoli, known for its beautiful Byzantine mosaics and stunning iconostasis. Built during the 19th century, the church combines Byzantine and Neoclassical architectural styles, making it a fascinating example of Syros' cultural blending.

Another significant Byzantine church is the Monastery of St. John the Baptist, located in the hills of Ano Syros. This tranquil monastery is surrounded by lush greenery and offers a serene setting for reflection and exploration. The church itself features an impressive Byzantine-style altar and is home to a number of religious relics. It's a perfect place for those looking to delve into the island's religious history while also enjoying the peaceful surroundings.

Many of these churches are still in use today, with local residents continuing to honor Byzantine traditions during religious festivals and ceremonies. Visiting these sacred sites offers not only an insight into the island's religious practices but also an opportunity to experience the deep spiritual connection that the people of Syros have with their history.

- **Specialty**: Byzantine mosaics, religious relics, and peaceful monasteries.

- **Perfect for**: Spiritual seekers, history enthusiasts, and those wanting to experience the island's rich religious heritage.

Byzantine Pathways and Ancient Ruins: Connecting the Past

Beyond the churches, Syros' Byzantine pathways also lead to several ancient ruins and historical sites that trace the island's role in the Byzantine Empire. One notable area is the Ancient Fortified City of Syros, where the ruins of ancient walls, towers, and settlements provide evidence of the island's strategic importance during Byzantine times.

As you walk these ancient pathways, you'll encounter remnants of fortifications, watchtowers, and stone structures that once formed part of the island's defense system. These ruins are often hidden in the hills and valleys of Syros, creating a fascinating blend of history and natural beauty.

Another important Byzantine site is the ancient theater of Syros, located just outside Ermoupoli. Though the theater itself is not fully intact, visitors can still make out the shape of the original seating areas and stage. The site provides a glimpse into the entertainment and cultural life of the island during its Byzantine occupation.

The beauty of exploring the Byzantine pathways of Syros is that many of the sites are relatively untouched, giving visitors the feeling of walking through living history. Whether you're tracing the ancient fortified walls or discovering hidden Byzantine relics, each step takes you deeper into the island's fascinating past.

- **Specialty**: Ancient ruins, fortifications, and historical sites.
- **Perfect for**: History lovers, archaeology enthusiasts, and those who enjoy walking through untouched historical sites.

Chapter 7
Amorgos – A Tranquil Escape

The Monastery of Hozoviotissa: An Aerial Sanctuary

Amorgos, the easternmost island of the Cyclades, is known for its natural beauty, tranquility, and striking landscapes. One of the most iconic and awe-inspiring landmarks on the island is the Monastery of Hozoviotissa, perched dramatically on the cliffs of the Chora area. This ancient monastery, built into the mountainside, offers not only a religious sanctuary but also one of the most breathtaking views in Greece. The Monastery of Hozoviotissa is a place where spirituality, history, and nature come together in harmony, creating a memorable experience for every visitor.

A Sacred Location

The Monastery of Hozoviotissa was built in the 11th century, during the reign of the Byzantine Emperor Alexios I Komnenos. It is dedicated to the Panagia Hozoviotissa, a famous icon of the Virgin Mary, believed to have miraculous powers. The monastery was originally constructed as a place of refuge for monks and pilgrims, and over the centuries, it has remained an important center of worship and religious life for the island's inhabitants.

Its location is nothing short of spectacular. The monastery is carved into the side of a steep cliff, nearly 300 meters above sea level, with a panoramic view of the Aegean Sea below. The setting is both serene and awe-inspiring, offering visitors a chance to connect with the divine while surrounded by the natural beauty of

Amorgos. The views from the monastery are absolutely stunning, with the turquoise waters of the sea and the rugged coastline stretching out before you.

The Architecture and Interior

The architecture of the Monastery of Hozoviotissa is a fascinating blend of Byzantine and Cycladic styles. The whitewashed walls of the monastery, the narrow corridors, and the small, hidden windows all contribute to the building's sense of peace and seclusion. The interior is just as impressive, with frescoes, icons, and a beautifully crafted iconostasis that give the space an aura of spirituality and reverence.

One of the most remarkable aspects of the monastery is its aerial position. To reach it, visitors must climb a series of stone steps that wind their way up the cliffs, providing spectacular views of the island's rugged terrain and the deep blue sea. The climb to the monastery is not for the faint of heart, but the reward is worth every step. Once inside, visitors can light a candle, pray, and take in the peaceful atmosphere of one of the most iconic religious sites in the Aegean.

A Place of Pilgrimage and Reflection

The Monastery of Hozoviotissa remains an active place of worship, with monks still living and praying here. Pilgrims visit the monastery every year, particularly on the feast day of the Panagia Hozoviotissa, which takes place on November 21st. On this day, the monastery is alive with religious ceremonies, and visitors from around the island gather to celebrate the Virgin Mary's icon and the miracles associated with it.

Whether you're drawn to the spiritual significance, the breathtaking views, or simply the sheer serenity of the place, the Monastery of Hozoviotissa is an experience that captures the essence of Amorgos. It's a sanctuary both in a literal and metaphorical sense, offering a peaceful escape from the world below.

- **Price Range**: Free entry, though donations are appreciated.
- **Specialty**: Byzantine architecture, panoramic views, spiritual atmosphere.
- **Perfect for**: History enthusiasts, spiritual seekers, photographers.

Beaches of Amorgos: From Agia Anna to Kalotaritissa

Amorgos, with its stunning landscapes and crystal-clear waters, is a true haven for beach lovers. Unlike some of its more tourist-heavy counterparts in the Cyclades, Amorgos offers beaches that remain largely unspoiled, each with its own unique character and charm. Whether you're looking for a quiet cove to relax in solitude or a more lively spot to enjoy the sea, Amorgos has a beach for every type of traveler.

Agia Anna Beach: The Iconic and Serene Retreat

One of the most famous and beloved beaches on Amorgos is Agia Anna, located near the village of Katapola. This beach gained international fame as the filming location for Luc Besson's 1988 film "The Big Blue", which showcased the island's breathtaking waters and rugged landscapes. The beach is relatively small but incredibly beautiful, with soft golden sand and crystal-clear blue waters that are perfect for swimming.

Agia Anna has a serene and peaceful atmosphere, making it ideal for those looking to unwind and relax in a picturesque setting. There are some beach bars where you can enjoy a refreshing drink, but the overall vibe remains tranquil and laid-back, with only a few visitors at any given time. The beach is surrounded by rocky cliffs, and the backdrop of the surrounding hills only adds to the sense of seclusion. The shallow waters are perfect for families, and there's plenty of space for lounging under the sun.

- **Specialty**: Soft sand, crystal-clear waters, famous filming location.
- **Perfect for**: Swimming, relaxing, enjoying nature, and film buffs.

Kato Akrotiri Beach: Seclusion and Natural Beauty

For those seeking a more secluded spot, Kato Akrotiri is a hidden gem located on the western coast of Amorgos. This small, pebbly beach is surrounded by cliffs and only accessible by foot or boat, which gives it an added sense of privacy and untouched beauty. The waters are pristine and perfect for swimming, with vibrant shades of blue and green that invite you to dive in and explore.

Kato Akrotiri is ideal for visitors looking to escape the crowds and enjoy the unspoiled beauty of the island. It's a great spot for snorkeling, with clear waters that reveal an underwater world filled with fish and marine life. Due to its remote location, there are no beachside amenities, so it's recommended to bring your own food, water, and sun protection for a day of complete relaxation.

- **Specialty**: Seclusion, crystal-clear waters, snorkeling.
- **Perfect for**: Quiet retreat, nature lovers, and adventurers.

Kalotaritissa Beach: A Peaceful Escape with Stunning Views

Located on the northwestern coast of Amorgos, Kalotaritissa Beach is another peaceful and scenic spot to explore. The beach is a combination of pebbles and sand, with shallow waters that are perfect for a refreshing swim. One of the most charming aspects of Kalotaritissa is its surrounding environment. The beach is Located within a cove and framed by steep cliffs, offering breathtaking views of the surrounding Aegean Sea and the nearby islands.

Kalotaritissa is located near the village of Kalotaritissa, which is known for its traditional Cycladic architecture and quiet atmosphere. The beach is not crowded, making it an ideal place for those seeking tranquility and relaxation away from the more tourist-centric areas of the island. Visitors can enjoy the serene atmosphere, watch the fishing boats in the harbor, or simply take in the beauty of the landscape.

The beach is also a great starting point for exploring the nearby Chozoviotissa Monastery and other historic sites on the island. Though it's a bit more remote, Kalotaritissa is easily accessible by car, and the winding drive through the island's scenic countryside adds to the charm of the experience.

- **Specialty**: Peaceful atmosphere, stunning views, nearby cultural sites.
- **Perfect for**: Relaxing, quiet retreats, and enjoying the landscape.

Agios Pavlos Beach: A Tranquil Gem with Shallow Waters

Another wonderful beach on Amorgos is Agios Pavlos, located near the village of Aegiali in the northern part of the island. This beach is known for its shallow waters and stunning surroundings. The sand is golden and soft, and the water is clear and calm, making it perfect for families and those who enjoy gentle swimming. The beach is relatively small, but it has a peaceful, untouched quality that makes it feel like a secret paradise.

Agios Pavlos is also known for the small chapel dedicated to Saint Paul, which is located near the beach. The chapel adds a touch of local spirituality to the beach, and it's a lovely spot to visit if you're interested in the island's religious history. In addition to relaxing on the beach, visitors can enjoy walking along the coastline and taking in the beautiful views of the surrounding hills and Aegean Sea.

While there are a few tavernas near the beach, Agios Pavlos maintains a more laid-back, rural atmosphere, making it perfect for those who want to experience the natural beauty of the island without the hustle and bustle of crowded tourist spots.

- **Specialty**: Shallow waters, local chapel, peaceful atmosphere.
- **Perfect for**: Families, relaxation, and cultural exploration.

Mikri Vlychada Beach: A Quiet Haven for Solitude

If you're looking for a beach that truly feels like your own private escape, **Mikri Vlychada** is a fantastic choice. This small, secluded beach on the southern coast of Amorgos offers clear waters and a serene environment, perfect for visitors who want to get away from it all. The beach is relatively hidden, with limited access, which contributes to its sense of tranquility.

Mikri Vlychada is ideal for those who want to enjoy the solitude of Amorgos' untouched coastline. There are no major facilities here, which only adds to the appeal for travelers seeking peace and quiet. The surrounding landscape of rocky hills and the deep blue waters of the Aegean create a picturesque setting that is perfect for unwinding and connecting with nature.

- **Specialty**: Seclusion, tranquil environment, untouched beauty.
- **Perfect for**: Solitude, nature lovers, and those seeking a private retreat.

Hiking Trails Through Wild Nature: A Nature Lover's Dream

Amorgos is a true haven for nature lovers and outdoor enthusiasts, offering some of the most scenic and **untouched hiking trails** in the Cyclades. With its rugged hills, deep valleys, and dramatic coastlines, the island provides the perfect environment for hiking, offering a variety of trails that range from easy walks to more challenging treks. Whether you're looking to explore hidden **coves**, visit **ancient monasteries**, or simply immerse yourself in the island's breathtaking natural beauty, Amorgos has something for everyone.

The Path to the Monastery of Hozoviotissa: A Spiritual and Scenic Journey

One of the most iconic hiking routes on Amorgos is the trail to the Monastery of Hozoviotissa. This ancient monastery, perched high on the cliffs, is one of the most important religious sites on the island and offers both spiritual significance and unparalleled views. The hike up to the monastery is a moderately challenging walk, taking about 30 to 40 minutes from the village of Chora.

As you ascend the trail, you'll pass through wild nature, with olive groves, steep hillsides, and stunning views of the Aegean Sea. The path winds its way through the rocky terrain, offering glimpses of the deep blue waters and the rugged coastline below. The final stretch of the hike takes you up a series of stone steps, leading directly to the monastery, which seems to emerge from the cliffs like a sanctuary in the sky. The sense of achievement when you reach the top, with the monastery in front of you and the incredible vista behind, makes this hike one of the most rewarding on the island.

- **Difficulty**: Moderate
- **Duration**: 30–40 minutes
- **Specialty**: Spiritual significance, breathtaking views, and the serene atmosphere of the monastery.
- **Perfect for**: Spiritual seekers, history lovers, and those looking for an easy but rewarding hike.

The Aegiali to Potamos Hike: Through Villages and Wild Landscapes

The hike from Aegiali to the village of Potamos is one of the most scenic and diverse on Amorgos. Starting in Aegiali, the trail takes you through traditional villages, offering a glimpse into the island's rural way of life, before heading into the wild, untamed nature that defines Amorgos' interior. Along the way, you'll pass through terraced fields, stone walls, and ancient olive groves, all set against the backdrop of the island's dramatic hills and coastlines.

The trail is moderate in difficulty and offers plenty of opportunities for breaks, whether you want to explore the charming stone houses of Potamos or enjoy the panoramic views of the surrounding valleys and hills. As you walk, you'll come across small chapels and ancient structures that speak to the island's long history, adding a layer of cultural exploration to the natural beauty.

Potamos is a tranquil village known for its laid-back atmosphere and scenic beauty, with winding streets, traditional tavernas, and stunning views of the surrounding hills. This hike offers an excellent combination of nature, culture, and history, making it a must-do for any hiker visiting the island.

- **Difficulty**: Moderate
- **Duration**: 1.5–2 hours
- **Specialty**: Traditional villages, olive groves, cultural and scenic beauty.
- **Perfect for**: Hikers looking for a mix of nature and culture, and those wanting to explore more of the island's rural life.

The Trail to Agios Pavlos: A Secluded Beach and Serene Views

For those looking for a peaceful and more remote hiking experience, the trail to Agios Pavlos offers a tranquil route through Amorgos' wild, rugged nature. This relatively easy trail begins from the village of Aegiali and takes you through the mountainous terrain, with beautiful views of the Aegean Sea and the small coves along the way.

The hike takes you to Agios Pavlos, a small, secluded beach known for its shallow waters and peaceful atmosphere. The beach is relatively quiet, with few visitors, and it's the perfect spot to relax after the hike, swim in the crystal-clear waters, or enjoy a picnic. The surrounding hillsides are covered with wildflowers, adding a splash of color to the landscape, and the view of the coastline from this secluded spot is truly spectacular.

The simplicity and seclusion of Agios Pavlos make this hike one of the most serene and rewarding on the island, especially for those who seek solitude and natural beauty.

- **Difficulty**: Easy to moderate
- **Duration**: 1–1.5 hours
- **Specialty**: Secluded beach, stunning views, and peaceful surroundings.
- **Perfect for**: Solitude seekers, beach lovers, and those looking for a quiet escape.

The Agia Anna to Kalotaritissa Trail: A Coastal Trek

The coastal trail from Agia Anna to Kalotaritissa is one of the most stunning hikes on Amorgos. This relatively long trail follows the coastline, offering hikers breathtaking views of the sea, cliffs, and the surrounding wild nature. The path winds through rocky terrain and wild shrubs, with occasional stops at secluded beaches and coves that provide the perfect opportunity to rest, swim, or enjoy a snack while surrounded by the beauty of the island.

The hike is moderate in difficulty, with some steep sections, but the incredible views and the sense of adventure make it an unforgettable experience. Along the way, you'll pass through wildflower fields, dense olive groves, and remote beaches, each offering its own quiet charm. Kalotaritissa, at the end of the trail, is a small village with a peaceful atmosphere, where you can enjoy a well-deserved meal or drink in one of the local tavernas.

- **Difficulty**: Moderate
- **Duration**: 3–4 hours
- **Specialty**: Coastal views, secluded beaches, wild nature.
- **Perfect for**: Hikers seeking coastal views, nature enthusiasts, and those looking for a longer trek.

Enjoying Amorgos' Slow Pace of Life

One of the most compelling reasons to visit **Amorgos** is its unmatched ability to offer visitors a break from the fast pace of modern life. Unlike some of the more tourist-heavy islands in Greece, Amorgos has managed to maintain its tranquil atmosphere, allowing you to truly disconnect, slow down, and embrace the island's relaxed lifestyle. The island's natural beauty, charming villages, and laid-back rhythms provide the perfect setting for a rejuvenating escape.

The Island's Timeless Rhythm

Amorgos is a place where time feels like it slows down. There's no rush to get from one place to another, and visitors are encouraged to embrace the **slow pace of life**. The island's main towns, **Chora** and **Aegiali**, retain much of their traditional character, with narrow streets, whitewashed buildings, and charming tavernas that serve as gathering spots for locals and visitors alike. The simplicity of life on Amorgos is apparent in the way people go about their daily routines—whether it's a leisurely coffee at a local café, chatting with friends in the village square, or enjoying a long meal at a taverna by the sea.

Walking through the **cobblestone streets** of **Chora**, you'll notice that the pace of life is unhurried, with no one rushing to be somewhere. People take time to greet each other, enjoy their meals, and appreciate the simple pleasures of life. The locals are friendly and welcoming, always happy to share a story or offer advice about the best places to visit on the island.

Savoring Local Flavors: Dining at a Relaxed Pace

One of the most enjoyable ways to immerse yourself in Amorgos' slow pace of life is by enjoying its **local cuisine**. The island's **traditional tavernas** serve dishes made with locally sourced ingredients, and dining here is a leisurely experience that invites you to relax, enjoy the food, and take your time. Whether you're sitting on a terrace overlooking the **Aegean Sea** or enjoying a meal in a village taverna, the experience is always about savoring every moment.

Amorgos' cuisine is simple but flavorful, with fresh **seafood**, locally grown **vegetables**, and island-made **cheeses** taking center stage. Be sure to try the **Naxian cheese, fresh fish**, and **lamb dishes** that are cooked to perfection. Meals are often accompanied by a glass of local **wine** or **ouzo**, and many tavernas offer their own homemade **desserts** such as **baklava** or **kataifi**.

As you dine, take in the surroundings—whether it's the sound of the **waves lapping against the shore**, the gentle **sea breeze**, or the warmth of the **sunset** as it paints the sky with golden hues. The pace is relaxed, and every meal is an opportunity to connect with the island's rich culinary heritage and enjoy the company of friends, both old and new.

- **Specialty**: Slow dining, fresh seafood, local wines, traditional Greek dishes.

- **Perfect for**: Food lovers, those seeking a relaxing dining experience, and anyone looking to savor the moment.

Taking a Leisurely Stroll: Exploring Amorgos at Your Own Pace

There's no rush to explore Amorgos, and part of the charm of the island is the opportunity to discover its beauty at a **leisurely pace**. Walking through the quiet villages, taking in the views of the rugged coastline, and exploring hidden coves and beaches allows you to fully appreciate the island's unspoiled landscape.

A leisurely stroll through **Chora**, with its narrow streets lined with whitewashed houses, is a great way to spend the day. The town's main square is perfect for people-watching, where you can sit at a café, enjoy a coffee, and soak in the relaxed atmosphere. Similarly, the **village of Aegiali** has a charming, small-town feel, where time seems to stand still. The harbor area is ideal for a peaceful walk by the water, with plenty of opportunities to stop at a taverna for a refreshing drink.

If you're feeling adventurous, explore some of the island's **hidden gems**—small **beaches**, quiet **hilltop villages**, or secluded **caves**—but always at your own pace. There's no pressure to rush or follow a strict schedule. The natural beauty of Amorgos is meant to be enjoyed in the slow, unhurried manner that the island embodies.

- **Specialty**: Peaceful walks, hidden beaches, charming villages.
- **Perfect for**: Slow exploration, nature lovers, and those looking to relax and unwind.

The Island's Slow Pace in the Evening

As the day draws to a close, the slow pace of Amorgos continues. The **sunset** on the island is a **magical time**—the sky is painted with soft hues of pink, orange, and purple, and the surrounding mountains and sea take on a serene, tranquil glow. The evening is the perfect time to sit at one of the island's many **outdoor cafes**, watch the sunset, and enjoy the quiet atmosphere that pervades the island.

The lack of nightlife noise or bustle gives Amorgos a peaceful, reflective feel. There's something special about watching the sun set over the **Aegean Sea**, with the soft sound of waves in the background, knowing that time here moves at its own pace.

- **Specialty**: Sunsets, quiet evenings, peaceful surroundings.
- **Perfect for**: Those seeking relaxation, couples, and anyone who wants to disconnect from the fast pace of modern life.

Chapter 8
The Lesser-Known

Ios: A Hidden Gem for Hiking and Beaches

Image by Johnny Africa on Unsplash

Ios is often overshadowed by its more famous neighbors in the Cyclades, like Mykonos and Santorini, but it remains a hidden gem for travelers seeking natural beauty, hiking opportunities, and stunning beaches. Known for its vibrant nightlife, Ios is also a destination that offers much more than parties and beach clubs. The island is quieter and more laid-back than its more famous counterparts, making it the perfect spot for those who want to experience the true essence of the Greek islands without the crowds.

Hiking in Ios: Exploring the Island's Rugged Terrain

Ios is a hiker's paradise, offering a range of trails that explore the island's rugged landscapes, hilltop villages, and remote beaches. The island's terrain is diverse, with steep hills, rocky paths, and breathtaking views of the Aegean Sea, making it an ideal destination for outdoor enthusiasts. Hiking on Ios provides a unique chance to connect with nature while discovering the island's hidden gems.

One of the most popular hiking routes on Ios is the trail to the summit of Mount Pyrgos. The path leads you through traditional stone pathways, past olive groves and wildflower meadows, and offers panoramic views of the island's coastline and the nearby islands. Reaching the summit, you'll be rewarded with breathtaking views of Ios Town, the turquoise waters below, and the distant islands of Santorini and Naxos. It's a hike that's both scenic and invigorating, perfect for those seeking a sense of tranquility and isolation.

For those interested in more leisurely walks, the trail from Chora (Ios Town) to Manganari Beach is a fantastic option. This moderate hike offers glimpses of some of the island's most beautiful beaches, including Manganari, which is known for its soft golden sand and clear waters. Along the way, you'll encounter traditional villages, ancient ruins, and unspoiled natural beauty.

- **Difficulty**: Easy to moderate, depending on the trail
- **Duration**: 1 to 3 hours, depending on the trail
- **Specialty**: Panoramic views, rugged terrain, peaceful solitude

- **Perfect for**: Hiking enthusiasts, nature lovers, and those seeking quiet exploration.

Beaches of Ios: From Party Spots to Secluded Escapes

Ios is home to some of the most beautiful beaches in the Cyclades, with a range of options for every type of traveler. The island offers both lively beaches where you can enjoy beach bars and water sports, and secluded coves where you can find peace and solitude. Here are some of the must-visit beaches on Ios:

- **Mylopotas Beach** is one of the island's most popular beaches, known for its wide stretch of golden sand and crystal-clear waters. The beach is lined with **beach bars**, **restaurants**, and **water sports** facilities, making it a lively destination for visitors looking to enjoy a vibrant beach atmosphere. It's perfect for those who enjoy a bustling, social beach scene but still want to take a dip in the warm, inviting sea.

- **Manganari Beach** is another stunning spot, located on the southern coast of the island. The beach is more peaceful and remote, with soft sand, clear waters, and a relaxed vibe. It's an ideal location for swimming, sunbathing, and enjoying the unspoiled natural surroundings. The water here is shallow, making it great for families with children, and there are several tavernas offering fresh seafood just a short walk from the beach.

- **Agia Theodoti Beach** is a hidden gem, located on the northeastern side of Ios. This quiet, sandy beach is surrounded by rolling hills and cypress trees, providing a serene environment for visitors seeking a secluded escape. The beach is less crowded than Mylopotas and Manganari, making it a great place for relaxation and swimming.

- **Specialty**: Wide variety of beaches, from lively to secluded, crystal-clear waters
- **Perfect for**: Beach lovers, families, and those seeking a peaceful beach retreat.

Folegandros: Untouched Beauty and Hidden Coves

Folegandros is one of the most unspoiled and charming islands in the Cyclades, known for its rugged beauty, secluded beaches, and authentic atmosphere. Despite its proximity to more well-known islands like Santorini and Mykonos, Folegandros remains relatively undiscovered by mass tourism, offering a peaceful escape to those who seek a more authentic Greek island experience. The island's beauty lies in its untouched landscapes, its traditional villages, and its ability to transport visitors back to a simpler, slower time.

The Beauty of Folegandros Town (Chora)

The island's main town, Chora, is a picturesque village perched on the edge of a cliff, offering panoramic views of the Aegean Sea. Unlike the more crowded towns of other islands, Chora maintains a quiet, serene atmosphere. Its narrow, winding streets are lined with whitewashed houses, bougainvillea-covered walls, and charming cafes where locals gather to chat.

The town is characterized by its traditional Cycladic architecture, with little to no modern developments, creating a sense of timelessness. A stroll through Chora is like stepping into a postcard, with cobbled streets, tiny squares, and friendly locals who will greet you as you pass. At the highest point of the town is the Panagia Church, which offers stunning views over the island and is a great spot to enjoy a quiet moment of reflection.

Chora also boasts a vibrant local dining scene, with tavernas offering fresh, island-inspired cuisine. Don't miss trying local specialties like matoutou (a meat and vegetable stew) and louza (cured pork), served with locally produced wine or raki.

- **Specialty**: Traditional Cycladic architecture, panoramic views, quiet atmosphere.
- **Perfect for**: Peaceful exploration, dining, and photography.

Secluded Beaches: Hidden Coves of Folegandros

Folegandros may not have the large, crowded beaches of Mykonos or Santorini, but it more than makes up for it with its hidden coves and untouched beaches. The island offers a variety of beach options for every type of traveler—whether you're looking for peace and solitude or easy access to amenities.

- Agali Beach is one of the most popular beaches on Folegandros, but still retains a relatively quiet charm compared to more commercialized islands. The beach is surrounded by steep cliffs and offers shallow turquoise waters ideal for swimming and snorkeling. There are also a few beach bars and tavernas where you can enjoy a meal with a view of the Aegean Sea.

- Katergo Beach is a remote and isolated beach that is accessible only by boat or through a rugged hiking trail. The beach is small, with golden sand and crystal-clear waters that make it feel like your own private paradise. The hike to Katergo is an adventure in itself, as you'll pass through rocky terrain and wild landscape, but the reward at the end is definitely worth it. The absence of crowds adds to the charm of this pristine beach.

- Vardia Beach is another secluded spot, ideal for those looking to escape the crowds. Situated near the Old Castle, Vardia is a peaceful beach with crystal-clear waters and plenty of space to relax. While there are no facilities here, it's a great spot to bring a picnic, enjoy the scenery, and swim in the beautiful Aegean.
    - **Specialty**: Seclusion, pristine beaches, crystal-clear waters.
    - **Perfect for**: Beach lovers, those seeking solitude, and adventure seekers.

The Wild Nature of Folegandros: Hiking and Exploring

One of the best ways to truly appreciate the natural beauty of Folegandros is by hiking through its rugged landscape. The island is relatively small, but its terrain is varied, with steep cliffs, wild hillsides, and valleys that are home to native flora and fauna. Hiking here is a unique way to explore the island's hidden beauty, offering the chance to discover secluded beaches, charming villages, and ancient ruins along the way.

- The hike from Chora to Ano Meria is a wonderful way to experience Folegandros' wild landscape. The route passes

- through traditional stone villages, terraced hillsides, and offers panoramic views of the Aegean Sea. The journey is moderate in difficulty and is ideal for those who want to experience the island's untouched beauty.

- Another stunning trail leads to the Old Castle, a historic site that offers breathtaking views of the island and the sea. The ancient ruins are a reminder of Folegandros' long history, and the views from the site are some of the best on the island.

Folegandros is a dream destination for nature lovers and hikers. Its rugged landscapes and secluded beaches provide an opportunity for exploration, adventure, and connection with the natural world.

- **Difficulty**: Moderate to challenging, depending on the trail.
- **Specialty**: Rugged landscapes, hiking trails, panoramic views.
- **Perfect for**: Nature lovers, hikers, and those seeking adventure.

Serifos: A Remote Paradise for Adventurers

Serifos, a small and relatively untouched island in the Cyclades, is a true paradise for adventurers looking for a remote escape and a chance to immerse themselves in nature. The island's rugged landscape, crystal-clear waters, and secluded beaches make it an ideal destination for those who seek solitude, hiking, and exploring off-the-beaten-path destinations. Serifos has managed to preserve its traditional charm, making it a perfect choice for travelers who want to experience an authentic Greek island without the tourist crowds.

Exploring Serifos' Rugged Terrain: Hiking and Adventure

Serifos is a true **paradise for hikers,** offering a variety of trails that take you through the island's **rugged hills, wildflower-filled meadows**, and ancient villages. The island's diverse terrain provides both **challenging hikes** and more leisurely walks, all with spectacular views of the surrounding **Aegean Sea**.

One of the most popular hikes on the island is the **trail to the ancient mining town of Mega Livadi**. Serifos has a rich history in **mining**, and the trail to Mega Livadi offers a glimpse into this past. The hike takes you through **stone-built villages** and up to the **old mine shafts** that once thrived on the island. As you hike, you'll pass through **wild terrain** and **rocky paths**, but the views are breathtaking, and the opportunity to learn about Serifos' industrial heritage makes the hike even more rewarding.

Another incredible hiking trail leads to **Chora**, Serifos' charming capital, perched high above the island. The walk to Chora takes you through **breathtaking scenery**, past traditional whitewashed houses, and eventually up to the town's **old castle**. The castle provides panoramic views of the entire island and the surrounding sea, making it an ideal spot for photos and relaxation. The charming streets of **Chora** offer plenty of places to stop and enjoy the island's authentic atmosphere.

Serifos' rugged and wild landscapes are perfect for anyone looking for **adventurous exploration**—whether it's hiking to remote villages, exploring mining ruins, or simply enjoying the island's natural beauty.

- **Difficulty**: Moderate to challenging, depending on the trail.
- **Duration**: 1 to 3 hours, depending on the route.
- **Specialty**: Rugged landscapes, hiking trails, ancient ruins.
- **Perfect for**: Adventurers, history enthusiasts, and nature lovers.

Secluded Beaches: Tranquility and Natural Beauty

In addition to its dramatic landscapes, Serifos is home to some of the most **secluded and serene beaches** in the Cyclades. The island's beaches are perfect for those looking for a more private and peaceful experience, away from the busy crowds of larger islands.

- **Psili Ammos Beach** is one of the most beautiful and popular beaches on Serifos. Located on the southeastern coast, this sandy beach has **shallow, clear waters**, making it perfect for swimming and relaxation. The beach is relatively quiet and can be reached by foot or by boat. There are also a few beach bars where you can enjoy a refreshing drink after swimming. Its **seclusion** and natural beauty make it one of the island's top spots for a peaceful day by the sea.
- **Ganema Beach** is another stunning, remote beach located on the western side of Serifos. The beach is surrounded by **rocky hills** and has clear, turquoise waters that invite you to swim and snorkel. Ganema is perfect for those who enjoy a quieter atmosphere, as it is not as well-known as other

beaches in the Cyclades. You'll also find a couple of small tavernas here, offering fresh seafood and traditional Greek dishes. Ganema is ideal for a day of relaxation, with the added benefit of being far removed from the crowds.

- **Vagia Beach** is a small, quiet beach located near the port of Serifos. Though it's more accessible than other remote beaches, it still retains a peaceful, laid-back atmosphere. The beach is framed by high cliffs and **deep blue waters**, making it a perfect spot for swimming, reading, or simply unwinding with the sounds of nature.
    - **Specialty**: Seclusion, clear waters, peaceful atmosphere.
    - **Perfect for**: Swimming, snorkeling, and relaxation.

Exploring Serifos' Remote Villages: Authentic Island Life

Beyond its natural beauty, Serifos offers a rich cultural experience through its **traditional villages**. The island's villages are often overlooked by mainstream tourism, giving visitors the opportunity to experience authentic Greek island life. In these villages, you'll find **stone houses**, **narrow streets**, and **friendly locals** who take pride in their heritage and way of life.

- **Chora**, the capital, is the island's cultural and historical hub. Its narrow streets, whitewashed houses, and beautiful town square offer a glimpse into traditional island life. The **old castle** provides a fascinating historical experience, and the town is home to **local tavernas** and small shops where you can sample fresh, homemade Greek delicacies.

- **Livadi**, the main port of Serifos, is a small and charming village that offers beautiful views of the surrounding hills and beaches. The village is home to a few tavernas, cafes, and shops, making it a great place to unwind after a day of hiking or beachgoing. Livadi is also where you'll find the island's **mining heritage**, with old mine shafts and relics scattered throughout the landscape.

Serifos' villages are a place where you can slow down, enjoy a cup of coffee in a peaceful square, and chat with locals who are eager to share their stories and knowledge of the island.

- **Specialty**: Traditional villages, stone houses, island culture.
- **Perfect for**: Cultural exploration, authentic experiences, and connecting with locals.

Chapter 9
Practical Travel Tips for Cyclades Islands

Getting Around: Ferries, Boats, and Private Transfers

The Cyclades Islands are known for their picturesque landscapes, historical landmarks, and pristine beaches, but to fully enjoy the beauty of this island chain, it's important to understand how to get around efficiently. Whether you're island hopping between Santorini, Mykonos, Paros, or other lesser-known gems like Folegandros and Amorgos, the ferry system plays a major role in your travel plans. Additionally, boats, buses, and private transfers provide flexible ways to explore each island at your own pace.

Ferries: The Heart of Island Hopping

The most common and affordable way to travel between the Cyclades islands is by ferry. Ferries operate regularly from major ports like Piraeus (Athens' main port) and from other islands such as Santorini, Mykonos, and Paros. The Cyclades have an excellent ferry network, and the routes are generally well-connected. You can expect a smooth and scenic journey, with some ferries offering high-speed services that get you from one island to the next in just a few hours.

The ferry schedules can change depending on the time of year, so it's essential to book your tickets in advance, especially during peak seasons (June to August). During the off-season, ferries still run but might be less frequent. There are also overnight ferries that allow you to travel comfortably between the islands, saving both time and accommodation costs.

- **Major ferry companies**: Blue Star Ferries, **Hellenic Seaways**, and **SeaJets**.

- **Booking tips**: Book ferry tickets at the **port**, through **online platforms**, or at local travel agencies.

- **Travel time**: Ferry durations vary depending on the route—shorter trips can take **1–2 hours**, while longer journeys can take up to **5–6 hours**.

Boats: Exploring Hidden Coves and Remote Beaches

While ferries are ideal for island hopping, **boats** offer a more intimate and adventurous way to explore the smaller, hidden corners of the islands. Renting a private boat, or joining a **boat tour**, allows you to visit remote beaches, secluded caves, and scenic coves that are often inaccessible by land. The islands of **Milos**, **Amorgos**, and **Ios** are particularly known for their stunning coastline, and exploring by boat offers an unforgettable experience.

Boat rentals are available for **half-day** or **full-day trips**, and prices can vary depending on the size of the boat and whether you opt for a **self-drive** or **crewed boat**. **Skippered boat tours** are especially popular, where a local captain can take you to the best spots while providing insight into the island's history and culture.

- **Specialty**: Explore hidden beaches, secluded caves, and picturesque coastlines.

- **Price range**: €100–€500 per day, depending on the boat type and crew services.

Private Transfers: Comfort and Convenience

For those looking for convenience and a more comfortable experience, private transfers are an excellent option, especially for getting around on each island. Many islands offer private taxi services, shuttle transfers, and private drivers who can take you directly from the port to your accommodation or to specific destinations on the island. Private transfers are ideal if you're traveling with a group, carrying a lot of luggage, or just prefer a more relaxed experience.

On some islands, you can also rent a private car, scooter, or ATV, which provides flexibility and the ability to explore at your own pace. Rental companies are easy to find, and these modes of transport are perfect for exploring the island's hidden gems that may not be accessible via public transportation.

- **Specialty**: Convenience, door-to-door service, and flexibility.
- **Price range**: Private transfers can range from €20 to €100, depending on distance and type of service.
  - **Perfect for**: Travelers with limited time, those seeking convenience, or those with heavy luggage.

Best Time to Visit: Weather, Festivals, and Local Events

The Cyclades Islands enjoy a Mediterranean climate, characterized by hot, dry summers and mild, wet winters. The best time to visit depends on your preferences for weather, crowd sizes, and the types of experiences you're looking for. Whether you're after sunny beach days, local festivals, or a quieter atmosphere, the timing of your visit can greatly impact your experience in the Cyclades.

Weather in the Cyclades: Warm Summers and Mild Winters

- Summer (June to August): This is the peak tourist season in the Cyclades, especially in popular destinations like Santorini, Mykonos, and Ios. During these months, the weather is hot and dry, with daytime temperatures often reaching between 30°C to 35°C (86°F to 95°F). This is the perfect time for beach lovers and those seeking lively atmospheres with beach parties and vibrant nightlife. However, it's also the most crowded time of the year, with higher prices for accommodation and longer waiting times at popular attractions.

- Shoulder Season (May and September): If you prefer slightly milder temperatures and fewer crowds, visiting the Cyclades in May or September is ideal. The weather during these months is still warm, with temperatures ranging between 25°C to 30°C (77°F to 86°F), making it perfect for beach days and outdoor activities like hiking and exploring villages. You'll also enjoy a more relaxed vibe compared to the summer months, with prices for accommodation being more reasonable. September, in particular, is a great time to visit as the summer heat begins to taper off, but the sea remains warm for swimming.

- Autumn (October to November): The fall months bring a cooler, more comfortable climate, with temperatures ranging from 20°C to 25°C (68°F to 77°F). The crowds significantly thin out, and you can enjoy more peaceful beach days and sightseeing. While some tourist services may start to wind down in November, this is a great time to visit if you're looking for a quieter, off-the-beaten-path experience. However, expect occasional rain showers as the season progresses.

- Winter (December to February): Winters in the Cyclades are mild compared to other European destinations. Temperatures range between 10°C to 15°C (50°F to 59°F), with some rainy days. While many businesses and tourist sites close during this period, it's an excellent time for those seeking peaceful retreats and fewer crowds. Winter is also the best time to experience the island's local culture and enjoy its serene ambiance. Just be aware that not all ferry routes operate during the winter, and some islands may feel more isolated.

    o Perfect for: Beach lovers (summer), hikers and outdoor enthusiasts (spring/fall), peaceful retreats (winter).

Festivals and Local Events: A Taste of Cycladic Culture

The Cyclades are rich in cultural traditions, and the islands host a variety of festivals and local events throughout the year. From religious celebrations to cultural festivals, these events provide visitors with a deeper understanding of the islands' heritage and offer a chance to experience the authentic spirit of Greek life.

- Easter Celebrations (April): Easter is one of the most important holidays in Greece, and the Cyclades are no exception. Holy Week leading up to Easter Sunday is marked by processions, church services, and traditional celebrations. On islands like Syros, Mykonos, and Santorini, you'll find unique Easter customs, such as the lighting of candles, the ringing of church bells, and communal feasts. This is a great time to experience the islands' religious traditions and enjoy a sense of community.

- Festival of the Assumption of the Virgin Mary (August 15th): This is one of the most widely celebrated religious festivals in Greece. In the Cyclades, this event is marked by special church services, processions, and a festive atmosphere in many villages. Paros, Ios, and Syros are known for their particularly vibrant celebrations. It's a great time to visit if you want to experience the local culture and witness the islanders' deep spiritual traditions.

- Milos Festival (July to September): Held annually during the summer months, the Milos Festival features theater performances, classical music concerts, and art exhibitions. This is a fantastic event for culture lovers, offering a chance to see international artists perform in some of the island's most scenic venues. The Apollo Theater in Milos, with its historic charm, serves as a beautiful backdrop for many of these performances.

- Mykonos Summer Festival (June to September): Mykonos is well known for its lively nightlife, but during the summer, the island also hosts several cultural events. From open-air cinemas to art exhibitions, the Mykonos Summer Festival offers a mix of modern culture and traditional arts. Don't miss the chance to enjoy local music performances and theatrical productions while soaking in the island's world-famous atmosphere.

- Syros International Film Festival (October): If you're a film lover, the Syros International Film Festival is a must-see event. It's an emerging cultural highlight for the island, drawing filmmakers and movie enthusiasts from all over the world. The festival showcases a variety of films, including short films, documentaries, and feature-length movies, all set against the stunning backdrop of Ermoupoli.
    - Perfect for: Culture enthusiasts, festival-goers, and those interested in local traditions and celebrations.

What to Pack: Essentials for Island Hopping

When island hopping through the Cyclades, packing efficiently is essential to make the most of your trip. You'll be hopping between islands, often using ferries, boats, or small airports, so your luggage should be light, practical, and easy to manage. The climate, activities, and the diverse nature of each island also play a role in the essentials you'll need to pack. Here's a guide to help you pack smart and ensure you have everything you need for a smooth and enjoyable experience.

1. Light and Comfortable Clothing

Since the Cyclades have a Mediterranean climate, the weather is typically warm and sunny, especially in summer, with cooler evenings in the spring and fall. Here's what to pack for the best comfort:

- Breathable, lightweight clothes: Pack cotton, linen, and other breathable fabrics to keep you cool during the hot days. Light-colored clothes will also help keep you comfortable under the sun. T-shirts, tank tops, summer dresses, and loose-fitting pants are ideal for daytime.

- Swimwear: With so many beautiful beaches and crystal-clear waters in the Cyclades, swimsuits or bikinis are a must. Don't forget a cover-up or a sarong for walking to and from the beach.

- Layered evening wear: The evenings in the islands can be cooler, especially in April, May, and October, so pack a light jacket or sweater. A denim jacket, cardigan, or light sweater will be perfect for chilly evenings.

- Comfortable walking shoes: Most islands have cobblestone streets and uneven terrain, so comfortable shoes are essential for exploring. Flat sandals, comfortable sneakers, and water shoes (for rocky beaches or boat trips) will help you stay comfortable as you wander the islands.

- Sun protection gear: A wide-brimmed hat, sunglasses, and light scarves will protect you from the sun, especially when you're exploring outdoors or enjoying beach days.

2. Beach and Outdoor Essentials

The islands' natural beauty, combined with their abundance of beaches and hiking trails, makes packing for outdoor adventures important. Here's what you'll need to fully enjoy the Cyclades' stunning landscapes:

- Beach towels: Bring your own compact beach towel for lounging on the sand. Many beaches won't provide towels, so having one on hand is necessary.

- Snorkeling gear: If you're a fan of underwater exploration, pack snorkel gear (mask, snorkel, and fins). Many of the islands, such as Milos and Naxos, are known for their clear waters and excellent snorkeling conditions.

- Backpack or daypack: A small backpack or daypack is useful for carrying essentials while you explore. This is perfect for keeping your water bottle, sunscreen, camera, and snacks handy.

- Sunscreen: The Mediterranean sun can be intense, so pack a high-SPF sunscreen to protect your skin. Consider a reef-safe sunscreen if you plan to snorkel.

- Water bottle: Stay hydrated, especially during hot summer months. Carry a reusable water bottle that you can refill throughout the day.

- Hiking gear: If you're planning on hiking, especially on islands like Amorgos, Ios, or Folegandros, pack sturdy hiking shoes with good traction. A light rain jacket is also a good idea for occasional unpredictable weather.

3. Tech Essentials for Travel

The Cyclades are well-connected, but you'll still want to have your tech essentials ready for smooth travel, sharing photos, and navigating between islands:

- Smartphone and charger: A smartphone is essential for navigation, booking ferries, and finding places to eat. Don't forget your charger, portable power bank, and any adapters for the Greek power outlets (standard European 2-pin plug).

- Camera: The Cyclades offer countless photo opportunities with their scenic landscapes, beaches, and traditional villages. A camera or GoPro with extra memory cards will help you capture the island's beauty.

- Portable power bank: If you're spending long days exploring the islands, having a power bank is a lifesaver for keeping your devices charged, especially if you're relying on your phone for directions or photography.

- E-reader or book: For quieter moments at the beach or in a café, bring a light e-reader or a paperback book to relax with.

4. Health and Safety Items

While the Cyclades are generally very safe, it's always a good idea to carry a few essentials to ensure your trip goes smoothly:

- Prescription medication: If you take prescription medications, be sure to bring enough for the duration of your trip, as local pharmacies may not always have the specific medications you need.

- First-aid kit: A basic first-aid kit with band-aids, pain relievers, antiseptic, and any other personal medical needs will help you stay prepared for any minor injuries or discomfort during hikes or beach days.

- Bug repellent: While the Cyclades aren't typically mosquito-heavy, bug repellent can be helpful during the warmer months or in areas with dense vegetation.

- Sunglasses and lip balm: Protect your eyes and lips from the harsh sun with a good pair of UV-blocking sunglasses and hydrating lip balm with SPF.

5. Miscellaneous Essentials

Finally, there are a few additional items to make your trip to the Cyclades even more enjoyable:

- Travel guidebook: A guidebook or a well-curated travel app can help you find hidden gems, the best beaches, and dining spots, as well as provide historical context for the islands.

- Travel insurance: It's always a good idea to have travel insurance in case of unexpected changes to your plans or emergencies during your trip.

- Small purse or wallet: For exploring the islands on foot or enjoying a dinner out, a small crossbody bag or wallet can carry your essentials like ID, credit cards, and cash.

Local Customs and Etiquette to Know Before You Go

Understanding the local customs and etiquette in the Cyclades will enhance your travel experience, allowing you to immerse yourself in the culture while respecting the traditions of the islanders. Greeks are known for their hospitality, but being aware of their social norms will ensure that your visit is not only enjoyable but also culturally respectful. Here's a guide to help you navigate local customs and etiquette during your time in the Cyclades.

1. Greetings and Personal Space

- Greetings: The Greek people are generally very warm and welcoming. When meeting someone, it's common to greet them with a friendly "Kalimera" (Good morning) or "Kalispera" (Good evening), depending on the time of day. If you're visiting with a local or meeting someone for the first time, a handshake is typical, though close friends and family may greet each other with a kiss on both cheeks.

- Personal Space: Greeks tend to be more physically expressive than some other cultures, and personal space may feel closer than what you're used to, especially in crowded markets or small towns. However, it's important to remember that this is a reflection of their warmth and friendliness, rather than an invasion of privacy.

2. Dress Code

- Casual yet Respectful: The general dress code in the Cyclades is casual, but always try to dress modestly when visiting religious sites such as churches or monasteries. For both men and women, it's customary to cover your shoulders and knees when entering places of worship. Long skirts or pants and tops with sleeves are ideal. In some religious sites, you may be asked to cover your head, especially if you are entering a monastery.

- Beachwear: On the beaches, swimwear is acceptable, but it's important to cover up when leaving the beach or entering cafes, shops, or restaurants. It's considered impolite to walk around in a bikini or swim trunks away from the beach. Sunglasses and sun hats are also common in the Cyclades, but they should be removed when entering churches, monasteries, or homes.

3. Dining Etiquette

- Meals as Social Events: In Greek culture, meals are not just about eating—they're about sharing time and creating connections. When invited to a meal, be sure to arrive on time, as punctuality is highly valued. However, the pace of meals can be leisurely, and it's common to enjoy long, social dining experiences.

- Sharing Food: Greek meals are often served family-style, with dishes placed in the middle of the table for everyone to share. It's polite to sample all the dishes offered and be sure to try the local specialties. Don't hesitate to ask for recommendations, as the Greeks take pride in their culinary heritage. At larger gatherings, wait for the host to start the meal before you dig in.

- Offering Compliments: If the food is good, it's customary to compliment the host or chef. You may hear the phrase "Kali Orexi!" (Enjoy your meal!) as you begin dining, which is the Greek equivalent of "Bon Appétit."

- Drinking Etiquette: If you're invited to drink with a local, you may be offered raki (a traditional Greek spirit) or ouzo (an anise-flavored liquor). In social situations, it's customary to offer a toast before drinking, with the most common toast being "Stin Ygia Mas!" (To our health!). When drinking, it's polite to wait for others to raise their glasses before taking a sip.

- Tipping: Tipping in Greece is customary but not mandatory. In restaurants, rounding up the bill or leaving 5–10% is appreciated. Tipping taxi drivers and hotel staff is also common, though not as high as in some other countries. For bartenders, leaving a small tip for good service is always a nice gesture.

4. Respecting Traditions and Holidays

- Religious and Cultural Holidays: Greek Orthodox Christianity plays a central role in the lives of many islanders. Easter is the most important religious holiday, and you may encounter processions, church services, and festive gatherings. If you're on the islands during Easter, be mindful of the quiet reverence that the locals hold for the holiday, and respect the traditions. Assumption Day (August 15th) is another important religious celebration across the islands, with festivals, processions, and family gatherings.

- Siesta Time: In many smaller towns and villages, shops, cafes, and restaurants may close during siesta hours (typically from around 2:00 p.m. to 5:00 p.m.). This is a time for locals to rest and recharge, and while some businesses may stay open, expect a slower pace of life during the midday hours.

5. Photography Etiquette

- Asking Permission: When taking photos of people, especially in more rural or traditional areas, it's polite to ask for permission first. Many Greeks will be happy to be photographed, but it's always best to be respectful and considerate. If you want to capture locals at work, such as farmers or fishermen, make sure to ask for permission before snapping a photo.

- Religious Sites: Inside churches and monasteries, photography is often prohibited or restricted. Always ask for permission before taking photos in sacred places. Respect the quiet atmosphere of these sites and keep your voice low when inside.

6. Respect for the Environment

- Protecting Nature: The Cyclades are home to some of the most stunning natural landscapes in Greece, and it's important to respect the environment. Make sure to dispose of trash properly, avoid littering on beaches or hiking trails, and respect the island's wildlife. Conservation is a growing focus in the islands, and many locals are dedicated to preserving their natural beauty.

- Avoiding Disruptions: In more rural areas, you may encounter farm animals, such as goats or sheep, on walking paths or roads. Be mindful of your surroundings and avoid disturbing these animals or their owners.

Conclusion

The Cyclades Islands offer a diverse and unforgettable experience for every type of traveler. From the iconic beauty of Santorini's sunsets to the rugged charm of Folegandros' hidden coves, these islands provide a unique blend of rich history, stunning landscapes, and authentic Greek culture. Whether you're drawn to peaceful beaches, adventurous hikes, or immersing yourself in local traditions, each island has its own distinct personality, waiting to be explored.

Santorini, with its iconic cliffs and volcanic landscapes, offers a taste of luxury, romance, and history. Meanwhile, Mykonos provides the ultimate in glamour and nightlife, attracting those seeking vibrant social scenes and world-class dining. On the quieter side, islands like Naxos and Amorgos give visitors the chance to explore ancient ruins, hike through unspoiled terrain, and bask in the natural beauty that defines the Cyclades.

For those seeking a more off-the-beaten-path experience, islands like Ios, Serifos, and Folegandros promise peace, seclusion, and the perfect environment for disconnecting from the hustle and bustle of everyday life. From hidden beaches to local festivals, the Cyclades invite you to slow down, embrace their rhythms, and become part of their timeless charm.

Practical tips, from getting around by ferries and boats to respecting local customs and etiquette, will ensure that your time in the Cyclades is stress-free and filled with meaningful moments. The beauty of the islands lies not only in their breathtaking views but also in the warmth and hospitality of their people.

Whether you're embarking on a solo adventure, family vacation, or romantic getaway, the Cyclades offer an experience that stays with you long after you leave. Every corner of these islands tells a story—one of ancient traditions, breathtaking landscapes, and a slower pace of life that invites you to enjoy each moment fully.

Your adventure in the Cyclades awaits—so pack your bags, set sail, and create memories that will last a lifetime.

BONUS

5-Day Cyclades Islands Itinerary: Exploring the Beauty, Culture, and Tranquility

This 5-day itinerary for the Cyclades Islands will take you on a journey through some of the most beautiful and culturally rich destinations in the Aegean. Whether you're seeking natural beauty, local culture, or simply a relaxing escape, this itinerary offers a perfect balance of sightseeing, adventure, and relaxation. You'll visit Santorini, Mykonos, Ios, and Folegandros, covering iconic sights and hidden gems. This route is designed for those who want to explore the best of the islands while enjoying a leisurely pace.

Day 1: Arrival in Santorini – Iconic Views and Sunset Magic

- Morning:
    - Arrive in Santorini via ferry or flight.
    - Start your day by checking into your hotel in Fira or Oia—both towns offer spectacular views of the island's caldera and are ideal starting points for exploring Santorini.
    - After settling in, take a leisurely walk through the streets of Fira to get a feel for the island. The town is filled with boutiques, cafes, and stunning cliffside views.
- Afternoon:
    - Head to Akrotiri to explore the ancient Minoan city, buried by the volcanic eruption of 1627 BC. This archaeological site is one of the most significant in

Greece and offers a fascinating glimpse into the island's ancient past.

- o Afterward, relax and unwind at Red Beach, one of Santorini's most famous beaches known for its red volcanic cliffs and crystal-clear waters.

- Evening:
    - o Make your way to Oia for one of the world's most famous sunsets. Arrive early to secure a good spot along the caldera rim or from one of the many cafes with panoramic views.
    - o Enjoy a romantic dinner at a seaside taverna in Oia, where you can sample fresh seafood and local specialties while watching the sun dip below the horizon.

Day 2: Santorini – Wine, Villages, and Relaxation

- Morning:
    - o Begin your day with a visit to the Santo Wines Winery for a wine tasting experience. Santorini is famous for its unique Assyrtiko wine, and this winery offers both beautiful views and delicious local wine.
    - o After the tasting, visit the charming village of Megalochori for a peaceful stroll through its narrow alleys and traditional architecture.
- Afternoon:

- - Head to Pyrgos, a less crowded but equally stunning village. Climb up to the top of the Pyrgos Castle for panoramic views of the island, then enjoy lunch at a quiet taverna in the village.
  - Spend the afternoon at Kamari Beach, one of Santorini's black-sand beaches, where you can relax, swim, and sunbathe.
- Evening:
  - Enjoy a casual dinner in Fira or Firostefani—both towns offer fantastic restaurants with spectacular caldera views.
  - After dinner, stroll along the streets of Fira and enjoy the nightlife, with its lively bars, music, and open-air cafes.

Day 3: Mykonos – Glamour, Beaches, and Old Town

- Morning:
  - Take an early ferry to Mykonos (approximately 2 hours).
  - Upon arrival, check into your hotel and begin exploring Mykonos Town (Chora). Wander through the narrow streets lined with whitewashed buildings, and stop for a coffee in one of the town's charming cafes.
- Afternoon:

- - Head to Paraga Beach or Psarou Beach for a relaxing afternoon by the sea. Both beaches are known for their clear waters and vibrant beach clubs.
  - Alternatively, if you enjoy culture, visit the Archaeological Museum of Mykonos, which offers insights into the island's ancient past, or explore the Delos Archaeological Site (a short boat ride from Mykonos).
- Evening:
  - For dinner, enjoy the Mediterranean flavors at a seaside taverna in Little Venice, where you can enjoy views of the sunset as it sets over the water.
  - Later, experience the legendary nightlife of Mykonos. From glamorous beach clubs to cozy bars, there's something for everyone, whether you want to dance the night away or enjoy a quiet drink by the sea.

Day 4: Ios – Hiking, Hidden Beaches, and Relaxation

- Morning:
  - Take a morning ferry from Mykonos to Ios (about 1 hour).
  - Upon arrival, head to the Chora area, where you can enjoy a quiet morning walking through the narrow streets and traditional Greek homes.

- Visit the Panagia Gremiotissa Church for an excellent view of the island and surrounding coastline.

- Afternoon:
    - Embark on a hiking trail to the stunning Manganari Beach. The trail is moderately easy, taking you through rocky paths, offering beautiful views of the island's coastline along the way.
    - Spend the afternoon at Manganari Beach, known for its crystal-clear waters and relaxing atmosphere.

- Evening:
    - Enjoy dinner at one of the tavernas in Chora, offering delicious local cuisine like souvlaki or Greek moussaka.
    - End your day with a peaceful sunset at Agia Anna, the quieter, idyllic beach where scenes from *The Big Blue* were filmed.

Day 5: Folegandros – Untouched Beauty and Scenic Views

- Morning:
    - Take a morning ferry from Ios to Folegandros (approximately 1 hour).
    - Arrive in Chora, a picturesque village with narrow streets, whitewashed houses, and stunning views.

Spend some time wandering through this charming village and enjoying the relaxed atmosphere.

- Afternoon:
    - Hike to The Old Castle, where you'll have panoramic views of the island and the Aegean Sea. This spot is perfect for a peaceful, reflective moment and offers incredible photo opportunities.
    - Head to Katergo Beach, a secluded, pristine beach. You can get there by boat or a moderately difficult hike, but the journey is worth it for the untouched beauty and serenity of the beach.
- Evening:
    - Enjoy a dinner in Chora, where you can taste fresh seafood or local specialties like louza (cured pork) or matsata (local pasta with meat).
    - End the day with a quiet sunset on the cliffs above Chora, watching the sky turn shades of pink and orange.

Other Travel Guide By DexTravel

If you've enjoyed this journey, I invite you to explore my other travel guide books, each crafted to help you uncover the beauty and adventure of remarkable destinations. Whether you're dreaming of coastal escapes, desert wonders, or bustling cities, there's a guide to inspire your next adventure.

Each book is designed with the same attention to detail, insider tips, and passion for travel, ensuring you have all the tools you need for an unforgettable experience.

Simply scan the QR code to visit my Amazon Author Page and find all my books in one place.

How to Use the QR Code:

Open the camera or QR scanner app on your smartphone or device.

Point it at the QR code.

Tap the link that appears to be taken directly to my Author Page.

Thank you for your support, and I look forward to guiding you on your next adventure!

Printed in Great Britain
by Amazon